CLUBS TO CANNON

Warfare and weapons before the introduction of Gunpowder

by

Brigadier O. F. G. HOGG

C.B.E., F.S.A., F.R.Hist.S.
Sometime Assistant Master-General of the Ordnance,
War Office

Sometime Director of Technical and Military Administration,
Ministry of Supply

GERALD DUCKWORTH & CO. LTD.
3 HENRIETTA ST. LONDON, W.C.2.

First published 1968

© 1968 by O. F. G. HOGG

SBN 7156 0407 4 .

PRINTED IN GREAT BRITAIN
by Photolithography
UNWIN BROTHERS LIMITED
WOKING AND LONDON

PREFACE

Man has been afflicted by the curse of war since time immemorial and this survey attempts to show why this has happened, what weapons and countermeasures have been adopted over the ages and how struggles have been conducted in the past.

A complete history of warfare in all its aspects would be beyond compilation, so only a short study has been essayed.

I should like to express my gratitude to Mr. George Naish of the National Maritime Museum and Mr. J. H. Hopkins, Librarian of the Society of Antiquaries of London for their ungrudging help and advice in my task. I should also like to record my appreciation of the R.A. Institution for allowing me to quote from previous writings of mine which they have published.

OLIVER F. G. HOGG

Blackheath
Spring 1968.

TABLE OF CONTENTS

LIST OF ILLUSTRATIONS

LIST OF ILLUSTRATIONS

PROLOGUE

Ethologists tell us that there is an inborn urge to aggression in all creatures. This emotive force manifests itself in two ways; the impulse of the individual to guard his own particular territory and that of the tribe to secure its survival. The first is known as the *Territorial Imperative* and the struggle which occurs is always waged between members of the same species. Owing to an inherited behaviour mechanism this display of force is seldom, if ever, fatal. The aggressor, following the laws of his being, usually retreats after a certain amount of shadow boxing leaving the owner-occupier master on his own ground. The reason for this charade is a fundamental instinct in the animal or insect to preserve its species. If fights of this kind were to be carried to a conclusion, the lower orders of creation would in time be exterminated. Nature may be prodigal with her potential progeny but she is not so foolish as that. Generally speaking, clashes between different biological types do not take place and, except when hunger drives, animals hardly ever attack to kill. Murder as a pastime forms no part of the pattern of life. The tribe, if attacked, will naturally fight as a body for its existence.

Why have not these ancestral habits survived in man? Where has he gone astray during his evolutionary climb?

One could sympathise with a planetary observer if he came to the conclusion that human behaviour lacked reason. Such an onlooker, unaware of terrestrial instincts in general and of aggressive tendencies in particular, would be unable to understand world history as the diorama of happenings passed before his eyes. It would be a complete and utter enigma to him because the ever-recurrent pattern of phenomena would seem to be entirely devoid of explanation. To say that the course of history is shaped by human nature begs the question. If it be natural to engage in war for no specific reason, for religious fanatics to break one another's heads for the love of God, for politicians with similar views for their country's salvation to oppose each other so vehemently and for tyrants to drench the world in blood to save its soul, then this nature may be human but it cannot be said to be rational. Over the

13

centuries indoctrination has been so widespread that we have come to regard the perpetrators of such follies as leaders worthy of praise and are wont to rely on their political judgment. So attuned are we to this sorry state of affairs that most of us fail to realise just how stupid the historical mass behaviour of humanity has become.

When this realisation finally comes to pass, we are bound to ask ourselves why supposedly intelligent beings behave so irrationally. There must be some powerful factor at work, impervious to the lessons of experience and prudence, which blinds man's common sense so drastically. As Hegel says 'What experience and history teach us is this—that people and governments have never learned anything from history or acted on principles deduced from it'.

The answer to this question lies in the fact that human social behaviour, far from being determined by thought and culture, is still governed fundamentally by the laws of behaviour obtaining throughout the animal kingdom.

Man's greatest gifts, his faculties of ratiocination and speech, which have given him the mastery of the world, are not unmixed blessings, for the danger which threatens our civilisation with possible extinction is the result of his handiwork. His rapid development has conferred on him power over material resources at the expense of his instinctive behaviour mechanism which in his case was never very strongly developed. When man first appeared in the primeval forests there was little need for an inhibitory mechanism against slaughter. He was not particularly strong, he had no means of assault against his fellows save his hands and feet, and having neither fangs, nor claws, nor horns was not a potential danger to the rest of creation. His relations with his brethren must have been discreet rather than headstrong. At the dawn of humanity living space was unlimited; there was no shortage of natural food and no 'population explosion'. Man by nature, measured against the larger carnivores, must have been an inoffensive animal. Under such idyllic conditions fighting must have been the exception rather than the rule. As man evolved, however, he ate symbolically the fruit of the tree of knowledge and suddenly stumbled on the discovery of fire and mastered the technique of making artificial weapons. Crude they were but they gave him dominion over the beasts of the field. He thus became in a position to inflict fatal harm on his adversaries as his inhibitory mechanism was too weak to prevent violence. Killing as a means of power entered man's consciousness. Individual fighting led to tribal disturbances; warfare, *the art of massed attack and defence*, escaped from Pandora's box and it is still an ever-present hazard in human affairs.

It would of course be an abuse of language to apply the term *warfare* to the struggles of the early cave dwellers, but the germ was latent in man's soul. Aggression and its antidote—self defence —are, as we have shown, symptomatic of life and when elementary tribal organisations emerged and became consolidated, war reared its ugly head. Since that remote point in time the *Malady of Princes*, as Erasmus called war, has claimed many thousands of millions of victims. Not a record of which mankind can feel particularly proud.

The primitive assailant soon realised that striking at a distance conferred signal advantages; hence the universal custom of hurling objects with intent to kill or injure. These projective and propulsive urges, ranging from the flung stone to the intercontinental ballistic missile embrace four phases—manual, mechanical, explosive and thermonuclear; and these are closely associated with the four periods into which warfare may be divided—ancient, mediaeval, modern and future. No specific dates can be assigned to these periods as, not only do they overlap, but they fail to follow one another in chronological order; they merely indicate the degree of material progress reached by the peoples adopting their technique. For instance, the mediaeval and mechanical era was at its height along the shores of the Mediterranean long before the ancient and manual epoch had disappeared from Britain, and centuries after guns had been thundering in the west the tribes of backward lands were content to settle their arguments with shield and spear. Assuming, however, that the dates proposed refer to a community then in the forefront of development, the ancient period was approximately prior to 1000 B.C., the mediaeval period between 1000 B.C. and A.D. 1400, the modern period from A.D. 1400 to A.D. 1950 and the future period from A.D. 1950 to some impending date hereafter.

During the course of its existence warfare has undergone fundamental changes, since strategy, which determines its acts, is a living art subject to flux, in contrast to the principles of war which never alter. During recent centuries the result of this fluidity has been to suppress the more static forms of conflict and introduce mobility as a *modus operandi*. The tendency during the modern period, therefore, is for field operations to supersede massed confrontation. The mediaeval period was almost exclusively occupied with siege warfare though battles of movement did occur, particularly among nomadic hordes, and this period ushered in the classic age of sieges during which investment was regarded as one of the most potent instruments of fighting in the hands of a commander. Although struggles were waged in the open, the main features of a campaign and the hopes of the belligerents centred on the successful use of assault tactics. Military machines thus entered on their heyday.

Each of the four periods has its co-ordinated measures of attack and defence and to use the fortifications of one period as a defence against the weapons of another is to court disaster. Witness the fate of many of our castles in the Civil War and the inadequacy of the flimsy Japanese houses in an incendiary raid.

The following table gives these inter-relationships in detail:

Period	Phase	Weapons	Defence measures
Ancient	Manual	Personal	Shields, earthworks with palisades
Mediaeval	Mechanical	Engines of war	Armour, castles, walled cities
Modern	Explosive	Artillery Aircraft Rockets Armoured fighting vehicles	Redoubts, low-sited fortifications, trenches, concrete emplacements, defence works, fighter aircraft
Future	Thermonuclear	Guided missiles with atomic and thermonuclear warheads	Fighter aircraft, deep underground shelters, anti-missile missiles

War has thus travelled far from the club, stone, sling, bow and spear. As a factor in human affairs it has developed out of all recognition, but as a method of settling disputes it has entered the speedway of mass destruction. *Facilis descensus Averni.*

This volume treats with the first two periods of warfare—Ancient/Manual and Mediaeval/Mechanical—together with a concluding chapter describing the vast changes foreshadowed by the introduction of gunpowder.

CHAPTER I

PERSONAL WEAPONS

The development of personal weapons has been a long and gradual process. Acceleration at first was infinitesimal and ages passed before any signs of advancement became noticeable. This was followed by a prolonged period in which arms, although appearing to alter but little, did in fact improve very slightly in manufacture and design. It was only in the later stages of human history, when the rate of progress became more marked owing to man's increasing intelligence, ingenuity and skill, that new types continued to flower on the battlefield.

Personal weapons before the advent of gunpowder may be classified under three headings; those of the Stone, Bronze and Iron Ages. The first of these is normally divided into three stages:

The Paleolithic or Old Stone Age	Before 10,000 B.C.
The Mesolithic or Middle Stone Age	10,000 B.C.–5000 B.C.
The Neolithic or New Stone Age	5000 B.C.–2500 B.C.

To complete the dating table, the Bronze Age lasted from 2500 B.C. to 1000 B.C. and the Iron Age subsequent to 1000 B.C.

In considering early weapons, it must be stressed that these periods denote cultures rather than time charts, for they overlap in their application and often exist side by side in different parts of the world. For instance, there are some primitive tribes at the present day who still use fighting equipment belonging to the Stone Age. During the uphill struggle for a place in the sun there have always been peoples in the van of civilisation and it is to these in particular that the date-cultures indicated above apply.

The Old Stone Age covered an immensity of geologic time and during hundreds of thousands of years there was little sign of weapon improvement. The combatant of 500,000 B.C. could have easily been mistaken for his descendant 300,000 years later. The first weapon man fashioned was the club, not the polished knob-kerrie of the Zulu but the branch of a tree or a stump wrenched from the ground. Primitive though it was, it did at least afford our forbears the opportunity of settling disputes or acquiring from their neighbours pieces of property they coveted such as a better cave or a more attractive mate. During the millennia which followed, man managed to improve his original club by working on it with flint tools which he had in the meantime developed. The club, no doubt, had its uses but it did not enable its owner to strike at a distance, an indispensable asset in hunting or stalking human prey. Even the heaviest tree trunk was of little use in defence against the predatory denizens of the primeval forests or in attack on the fleeter animals required for food. Man therefore evolved the spear for throwing, the sling for hurling stones and the archaic bow for shooting. His spear was a wooden shaft the point of which had been hardened by fire. His arrows, too, were similar in shape though smaller, winged and barbed. With this improved armament, Stone Age man was better equipped to confront the animals he hunted and to slaughter the fur-bearing mammals required for his sartorial adornment.

Later on, Paleolithic man became a prehistoric sculptor by learning to chip stones to his liking. He gradually became more adept at this art and was thus able to shape his material to obtain a good cutting edge. Experience taught him that obsidian and flint produced the best results because they would flake when struck. He therefore expended time and energy in searching for these desirable minerals for to his simple mind they were a prize worth seeking. In this manner he was able to construct tools which in turn enabled him to extend his armoury. Now, not only did he have flints and wood for his purposes, he had also bone, horn and ivory which he obtained from his forays. He was thus slowly and painfully climbing the evolutionary ladder towards eminence in the battle of life. Craftsmen in the Middle Stone Age in their quest for new horizons conceived the idea of lashing their flint instruments to wooden handles by means of animal tendons and strips of raw hide gathered in the chase. This was a notable advance, placing the stone club, the stone-tipped spear and the flint arrowhead at man's disposal. This method of attachment, however, had its drawbacks; it was not universally satisfactory and lacked the security which the use of such weapons demanded.

Men of the Later Stone Age improved on this technique by learning, through the alternate application of heat and water, to drill holes in flints into which wooden shafts could be driven. Armed with these more sophisticated appliances, man began to assume a more assured place as a warrior.

The Bronze Age ushered in the sword and the dagger. Copper, the main constituent of bronze, was formerly widely distributed though it is now mined only in territory where its extraction is a commercial proposition. It was in use in Britain nearly 4,000 years ago. Countries in the ancient world during the second millennium before the Christian era converted it into bronze by mixing it with tin. The drawback of pure copper as a material for arms is its ductility. Being soft, it keeps neither its shape nor its edge. Alloyed with 15 per cent of tin, however, it becomes a hard bronze capable of taking a cutting edge and has to a large extent the property of resisting oxidisation. Tin, therefore, became an important article of commerce in biblical times and the Phoenicians exploited it in Britain, particularly in Cornwall where supplies were plentiful. Early smiths toughened the edges of bronze weapons by repeated cold hammering on an anvil as the alloy tends to soften when cooled quickly after heating. Bronze can be cast into any requisite shape by suitable adaptations in the moulds, and thus sockets in the heads of weapons to take the necessary shafts could be easily produced. This led to simplification in the making of spears, arrows and battle-axes—arms which proved far superior to their prototypes of the Stone Age.

The discovery of bronze, therefore, introduced a new chapter in weaponry. The original knife-blade of the Bronze Age grew longer and narrower as time passed and eventually developed into a new weapon—the sword. The earliest swords were fashioned for thrusting like the modern rapier; the sabre or heavy cutting sword being a later development. The Iron Age continued the work which the Bronze Age inaugurated. Iron was a stronger and harder material than bronze and had better qualities for the work it had to undertake when adapted to the soldier's needs. Its main drawback is its liability to rust in damp air, a characteristic which modern science has successfully overcome. The Iron Age multiplied and perfected the types of swords and spears and introduced many new arms such as the pike, the lance, the gisarme, the halberd, the partizan and the like. The reign of all these has been brought to a close by the advance of artillery, except the sword and the lance which lingered on till the 20th century, and the dagger which still haunts our nightclubs.

The history of weapons and their countermeasures is part and parcel of that of man in all ages and in all climes. It unfolds the unceasing competition between the methods of attack and defence. This age-old struggle is independent of time or weapon. The shield was introduced to guard against the sword, the arrow and the spear. Armour was developed to save its wearer from the effects of the lance, spear, sword, arrow and cross-bow bolt. The armour-piercing shell was designed to defeat the armour plating of ships and the A.B.M. system has been invented to neutralise the intercontinental ballistic missile. As every civilisation harbours its own seeds of decay so does every new form of armament contribute its own antidote. It is the rhythm of life, the everlasting systole of war; and as scientific achievement advances we shall get more and more involved in this merry-go-round till at last life and death will stalk hand in hand through a poisoned world.

The prototypes of most of the personal weapons of the manual and mechanical periods had already appeared during the Iron Age and these may be classified as:

Cut and thrust—Sword, dagger
Staff—Spear, lance, axe, etc.
Concussion—Club, mace, flail, etc.
Missile—Sling, bow, long bow, blow gun and cross-bow

The sword holds a unique place among personal arms. It symbolises the State, justice and power. Together with the spur it is the emblem of knighthood. No other weapon has been accorded such favour and none has been treated with more respect. Magical properties have even been attributed to the swords of famous warriors in legend and history. Yet, notwithstanding all the literature devoted to it, the sword is a comparatively late arrival in man's armoury. Developed from the bronze dagger, it was strengthened by passing the blade through the hilt by means of a tang. This improvement was appreciated early in its development and has over the centuries become a universal practice. Many types of sword have come into being during the last 4,000 years as each community evolved the pattern most suitable to its needs. The original bronze swords were cast with a leaf-shaped blade, pointed and edged on both sides. The hilt was small and the blade short rather like the modern bandsman's weapon. The Iron Age introduced the forged blade as iron under heat was capable of being hammered into shape. The hilts, however, were still usually made of bronze which in special cases were highly ornamented with precious metals. In Europe, the straight sword was favoured except for mounted troops who used those of a curved type. The latter cuts more easily as it meets its victim obliquely allowing the blade to act as a saw. Non-European races, on the other hand, preferred the curved pattern. The number of oriental swords is legion and it would be quite impossible to list the various types—scimitars, yataghans, shamsirs and tulwars—which proliferated in various parts of Asia and Africa. Broadly speaking, the nations of the near east and central Asia tend to have curved swords whereas those of the far east, like Japan, have swords with straighter blades.

The Greeks used two kinds of sword, the leaf-shaped *akinakes* and the curved *kopis*. The latter form re-appeared among Spain's iron age weapons as the *falcata*. The Roman sword originally followed the normal Iron Age pattern. It was broad, straight and double-edged, the hilt and quillons being formed by globular protuberances. In the later days of the empire troops used the longer *spatha* of the barbarians. The Byzantine sword was broad and short, the hilt often being eagle-headed. The Viking sword played an important part in the history of this weapon. It succeeded earlier Scandinavian patterns and was the true forerunner of the mediaeval knightly weapon which is so often portrayed in effigy on tombs. The blade was finely tempered as the Vikings had learned the art of carbonisation. It was balanced when held by the addition of a heavy triangular pommel at the end of the grip and the hand was protected by short quillons. The hilts were often intricately inlaid. The blade was straight, two-edged and long, having a channel down the centre to give lightness and increased strength. The Bayeux tapestry shows that the Normans carried this type of sword with a simple cruciform hilt. Just before the advent of gunpowder the two-handed heavy sword made its appearance. In the Middle Ages, the sword was used in close fighting after the broken lance had been discarded during the first charge. At the same time, a special stiff thrusting sword with no cutting edge, known as the *estoc*, was introduced to pierce the armour of unseated knights.

The sword may be summed up as a simple weapon consisting of a sharp blade, a hilt and a cross-guard and pommel, appearing in an almost bewildering number of guises.

The dagger, preceding the sword, is found in all parts of the world and is probably the most common form of personal weapon. It is short, sharp and lethal in its effects. It was employed by early Iron Age man and is still in use today by the commando, for a quick stab above the kidneys is fatal. For this reason it is a favourite weapon among gangsters, for it is silent and deadly. It is almost indistinguishable from the knife. Examples are the Afghan knife, the Gurkha *kukri*, the Malayan *kris*, the Japanese *tanto* and the *barong* from Borneo. Some of the examples were finely damascened and beautifully engraved. Its main object was to deliver the *coup de grâce* and in this it was highly successful. The poniard, misericorde, dirk and stiletto are variants from the same stable and are used for the same purpose. The *dagger* must not be confused with the old English word *dagg* which was a form of pistol.

The spear is one of the earliest and simplest of weapons. Beginning life as a sharpened stick it has persisted among primitive peoples down to the present day. The head of the Bronze Age spear varied considerably in size and shape; sometimes broad and flat, at others long and triangular. The javelin is a shorter version of the same weapon. The Egyptians employed the javelin except when fighting on board ship when they used large daggers. The original Greeks carried two spears, a short one for stabbing and a long one for throwing; a practice still obtaining among the Zulus and other African tribes. The *pilum* or short spear of the Roman legionary was used both as a throwing spear and a javelin. The long spear eventually became the principal weapon of the foot-soldier in the Middle Ages. It was sometimes furnished with a short cross-piece below the head. This developed into the pike of the 16th century. The lance was a specialised form of spear employed by cavalry. It remained light and comparatively short, being wielded loosely by hand, till the introduction of the stirrup into Europe by the Huns under Attila enabled the knight to obtain a firm grip in the saddle and carry a heavier lance which he could couch under his arm. This improved weapon had a pointed head of steel and a circular vamplate to protect the hand, the shaft being built up in longitudinal sections with an increase in diameter fore and aft the grip. These lances being exceptionally heavy required a rest to be fitted to the right side of the knight's breastplate.

When cutting as well as thrusting became an article of faith on the battlefield, a host of staff weapons appeared among troops. The chief examples were the bill, the glaive, the gisarme, the war-hammer, the battle-axe, the pole-axe, the halberd, the partizan, the ranseur and the voulge.

The bill or war-scythe—a peasant weapon—was adapted from the agricultural implement of the same name, the single-edged cutting blade being incurvated so that the point turned towards the sharp edge. There were several variations in design ranging from crooked heads to vicious-looking straight scythes. Some having a blade over four feet long were used by the *Tschaikists* of Austria to mow down the crews of hostile boats. These particular troops derived their name from the river Tschaike.

The glaive or scythe-knife—a modified form of bill—has the point of its single-edged blade curving away from, instead of towards, its cutting edge. The point itself is double-edged and there is a hook at the base of the blade for enabling the foot-soldier to grab his mounted adversary by the neck or belt and pull him from the saddle. Left helpless on the ground the unfortunate rider fell a victim to the *estoc*.

The gisarme is somewhat similar to the glaive and the bill but it differs from them in being double-edged and armed with hooks. It dates from the Bronze Age and was in use among the Celtic and Germanic tribes. Its French name is attributed to the *guissards*, followers of the house of Guise who were armed with this particular weapon. Olivier de la Marche, a French chronicler born in 1426, maintains that the gisarme was of great antiquity having originated from the practice of fastening a dagger to a battle-axe.

Weapons of the axe-type include the war-hammer, the battle-axe, the pole-axe, the halberd, the partizan, the ranseur and the voulge.

The war- or pole-hammer was well known in Germany under the name of *Luzerner Hammer* as it was a favourite weapon with the people of Lucerne. It was called the pole-hammer in England because the spiked hammer-like head was fixed to a long pole. It had an unbroken descent from the elementary form which existed during the Stone and Bronze Ages. Charles Martel, the grand-father of Charlemagne, owes his name to this formidable weapon, the use of which became universal in Europe during the Middle Ages. Some of these war-hammers were veritable instruments of death, that of Tommelin Belefort weighing 25 lb. The short-handled hammers which knights were wont to carry along with the mace at their saddle-bow were almost as old as the pole-hammer. There are some bas-reliefs in the Louvre which depict Amazons attacking their enemies with a short-handled double-edged war-hammer.

The battle-axe evolved directly from the flint-headed axe of the Stone Age. It was made up of an axe-head of bronze, and after-wards of iron or steel, fixed to a handle. When the length of the handle was increased to about five feet it became transformed into the pole-axe. It was a popular weapon among the Germanic tribes who developed it from the domestic hatchet. At the battle of Hastings, the Saxons gained an initial success over the Normans with their pole-axes and, as a result, there were many casualties among William's followers. Battle-axes have assumed many forms but the principle of the weapon has remained constant—to cut and thrust in single combat. Just prior to the introduction of gun-powder, the soldier's battle-axe underwent a revolutionary change by incorporating the war-hammer, a take-over bid in the mediae-val armament world. Thus, though it still had an axe on one side it had a point or a large curved saw-edge on the other. By this double-purpose combination its efficacy was enhanced.

The halberd was a much later development, appearing on the battlefield only at the same time as the primitive cannon. It was a combination of spear and axe. The Swiss halberd was instrumental in winning the battle of Sempach in 1386. The partizan also made a late bow on warfare's stage. The term covered a number of forms including the ranseur which originated in Corsica. All had symmetrical heads either with a spike inserted between two axe blades or with a broad pointed blade with a pair of flukes at the base. Two centuries after their introduction both the halberd and the partizan retired from active service and became symbols of authority. They are now only used by members of royal bodyguards, such as the Yeoman Warders of the Tower of London. When employed as emblems of pageantry they are usually beautifully etched and gilded, their staves being adorned with silken tassels.

The voulge was a weapon greatly in use among the ancient Swiss. It was a broad-bladed, long-hafted implement sometimes incorporating a hook.

Outside Europe, weapons of the staff class assume many different forms some of which are very bizarre, having heads carved to represent men and birds. The simplest is the tomahawk of the American Indian which could be employed as a hatchet or throwing axe. India, Japan and the South Sea Islands contribute their quota of war-axes and the Maori of New Zealand possesses the greenstone *meri* which is undoubtedly an excellent skull-cleaver.

The third class of personal weapon, the concussive, relies on the weight of blow for its effect. When hit on the head the victim is either stunned or killed. Such weapons are by their very nature those of primitive man, as they derive from the primordial club which has no cutting or thrusting qualities. The discovery of metals improved the original club and details such as the insertion of iron spikes could be added to enhance their performance. The loaded club and the stone hammer became the more sophisticated mace, this name being derived from the Latin word *massa*. Roman soldiers are known to have carried round-headed maces and the weapon is shown more than once on the Bayeux tapestry. By the 13th century the mediaeval mace-head having developed flanges had assumed the characteristic form it retained till its disuse 300 years later. The weapon, now an instrument of civic authority, is at present used solely on ceremonial occasions. Each borough council has its mace, so does the House of Commons. The knight carried his mace at his saddle-bow and usually took it into use when his sword had been broken or lost.

The morning star is a form of mace the head of which bristles with spikes. It was commonly used as it was easy to construct by driving nails into a cudgel. It was thus a popular arm among the peasantry of Europe. The military flail or holy-water sprinkler was also a form of mace. It consisted of a shaft containing several

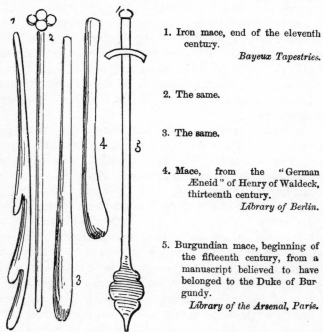

1. Iron mace, end of the eleventh century.

   Bayeux Tapestries.

2. The same.

3. The same.

4. Mace, from the "German Æneid" of Henry of Waldeck, thirteenth century.

   Library of Berlin.

5. Burgundian mace, beginning of the fifteenth century, from a manuscript believed to have belonged to the Duke of Burgundy.

   Library of the Arsenal, Paris.

Fig. 1.—Examples of the mace.

whips made of chain, each ending with a studded ball. It was introduced about the time of the Norman conquest and was well known in Germany and Switzerland during the two succeeding centuries. It was, however, little used, possibly because it was far from accurate unless wielded by an expert. It was more popular as a weapon in Russia and Japan than in western Europe.

The sling was man's first missile weapon. It was made of two long strips of pliable hide, sinew, leather or cord, one end of each strip being attached to the sides of the pouch which held the stone. The slinger released his missile by twirling the weapon round and round his head to gain momentum and letting go one strip at the psychological moment. The Bible recounts the duel between David and Goliath, the youth and the Philistine giant, in which the former

6. English mace, in wood and iron, reign of Henry V. (1413—1422).

Meyrick Collection.

7. English mace, in iron, middle of the fifteenth century.

8. German mace, fifteenth century, engraved iron; it is about 22 inches in length, and has the handle wired.

Arsenal of Lucerne.

9. Turkish mace, iron, fifteenth century; an architectural rose is damascened in the top.

Musée d'Artillerie, Paris.

10 A. Mace, from a manuscript of the end of the fifteenth century, being a copy, illustrated with numerous miniatures, of the *Schah - Nameh* or royal book, composed by the poet Ferdusi in the reign of Mahmoud (999).

Library of Munich.

10 B. The same.

11. French mace, sixteenth century.

Fig. 2.—Examples of the mace.

used the sling to good effect. The range of the sling in the hands of an expert was approximately 500 yards under suitable weather conditions. The Egyptians, Greeks, Romans, Persians and others had companies of slingers enrolled in their armies. The use of this weapon was discontinued in Europe about the 16th century. Savage tribes, however, have always shown great partiality for the

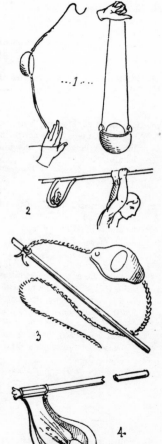

1. **Two** illustrations of slings, one with the thong loosened, the other with both thongs held in the slinger's hand; from a tenth-century manuscript.

2. Slinger with his staff sling, from a manuscript of Mathieu Paris, an English chronicler, born at the end of the twelfth century, died in 1259, who was the author of a *Historia Major Angliæ* from 1066 to 1259.

3. Staff sling from a manuscript of the beginning of the fifteenth century.

   Ambras Collection.

4. **Long-shafted** staff sling, intended to hurl grenades. From a manuscript of the sixteenth century.

   Library of the Chevalier von Haus-laub at Vienna.

Fig. 3.—Slingers and slings.

sling and are extremely adept in its use. Although not strictly a sling, the *bola* of the Patagonian Indians belongs to the same class of weapon. It consists of two round stones connected by a leather thong. The manipulator swings the contraption in circles round his head and, aiming at his target, releases it. The rotating bola entangles itself round the legs of its victim rendering him temporarily helpless. The boomerang of the Australian aborigine is another form of missile weapon which when thrown up wind can be made to return to its owner should it miss its target.

The blow-gun or blow-pipe is another primitive weapon which can cause havoc when used with precision especially when its dart is dipped in curare or some other active poison. It consists of a long hollow tube into which a small feathered dart is inserted. The 'breech end' is placed in the mouth of the native and a puff of air from his lungs sends the deadly missile on its way. The range is not great but its effect is almost instantaneous. It is a favourite weapon of the African pygmy and the South American Indian, and in mediaeval times was employed to shoot poisoned arrows, Greek fire and small shot.

The bow is universal and has been in use since the Stone Age, flint arrow-heads from Neolithic times having been found in large numbers. It consists of an elastic piece of wood or metal slightly depressed in the centre from the ends of which a tensioned cord is stretched. The arrow is a clean shaft of wood pointed and barbed at one end and feathered at the other to procure stability in flight. It is remarkable that the ancients, though they had no conception of external ballistics, should have realised that to increase velocity and therefore range it was essential to impart rotational velocity to an elongated missile. To fire, the arrow is held by the left hand at the centre of the bow and the cord is pulled back to the chest by the right hand thereby putting the bow into a greater state of compression. On releasing the cord the weapon regains its shape and propels the arrow towards its target. The Cretans, Scythians, Persians, Thracians and Parthians were just as celebrated in their day for their prowess with this weapon as were the English in Plantagenet times. The Romans, strangely enough, did not develop the bow but relied on their mercenaries to supply the deficiency.

William the Conqueror used his archers to good effect at the battle of Hastings but their pattern was the short bow. The long bow did not reach its apex in England till the end of the 13th century when the English archers decimated the Scottish spearmen at the battle of Falkirk on 22nd July 1298. It was the supremacy of the bowmen of England which gave this country her victories in the Hundred Years War. The English long bow was made of yew and was six feet in length, the arrow being one yard long. Practice and skill as well as muscular strength were needed to use this weapon effectively. A good archer could discharge six aimed shafts a minute with an effective range of up to 240 yards and a maximum range of 340 yards. It was the massed fire of the archers on a battlefield which proved so devastating to opposing troops. The great advantage of the long bow lay in its cheapness and simplicity. It had no mechanism to go wrong and required no special ammunition. Even after the introduction of firearms the long bow still retained its pride of place and remained current armament in England till the reign of Elizabeth I.

Oriental bows are quite distinct from the English long bow in that they are shorter, more powerful, have a longer range and employ a different principle. They were used by the Turks, Parthians, Indians, Persians, Tartars and Chinese. As all these different weapons are somewhat similar in design, the Turkish bow will be described as representing the general pattern.

The statistics of the Turkish bow were as follows:

Length	3 feet 9 inches
Length of bow string	2 feet 11 inches
Greatest width of each arm of the bow	1·125 inches
Thickness of each arm at a distance of 6 inches from the centre of the handle of the bow	$\frac{1}{2}$ to $\frac{3}{4}$ inch
Circumference of each arm at a distance of 6 inches from the centre of the handle of the bow	3 inches
Weight of bow	12 oz.
Pull of the bow	118 lb.

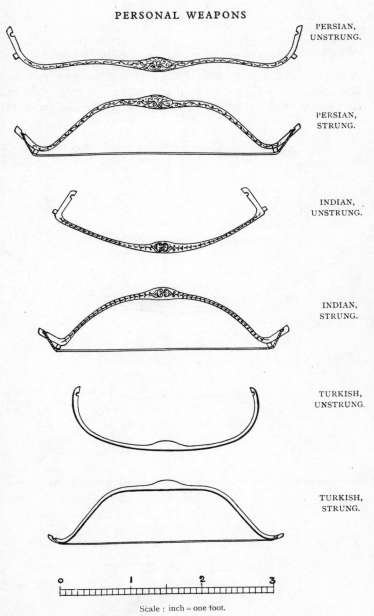

PERSIAN,
UNSTRUNG.

PERSIAN,
STRUNG.

INDIAN,
UNSTRUNG.

INDIAN,
STRUNG.

TURKISH,
UNSTRUNG.

TURKISH,
STRUNG.

Scale : inch = one foot.

Fig. 4.—Examples of oriental bows.

| Length of the arrow | 25 inches |
| Weight of the arrow | 7 drams. |

The bow is mainly constructed of very flexible horn and sinew. These materials, softened by heat and water, are glued longitudinally to a slight lath of pliant wood. This strip of wood formed the

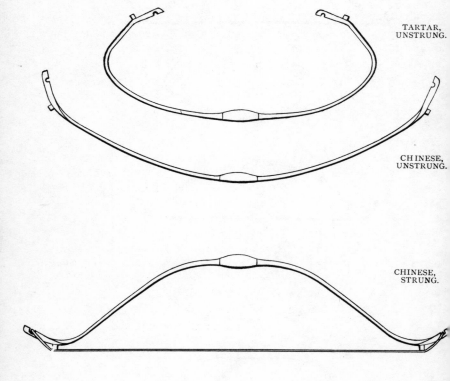

TARTAR,
UNSTRUNG.

CHINESE,
UNSTRUNG.

CHINESE,
STRUNG.

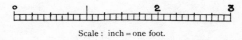

Scale : inch = one foot.

Fig. 5.—Examples of oriental bows.

core of the bow and extended for three inches beyond the strips of horn and sinew at both ends and slightly overlapped them. The projecting ends of the wooden core are enlarged to join the solid extremities of the bow in which nocks are cut to accommodate the ends of the bowstring. The two curved horn strips which in part comprise the arms of the bow are cut from buffalo or antelope horn and average about three quarters of an inch in thickness. The thicker ends of these pieces meet at the middle of the bow handle. The sinew which forms the back of the bow is taken from the great neck tendon of the ox or stag. This is shredded longitudinally and, after being soaked in elastic glue, is compressed into a long flat strip about a quarter of an inch thick, moulded into a pliable state to the wooden core and glued to it. It thus forms the back of the bow when bent. The bark of a cherry tree or a piece of leather or skin is next glued over the sinew to preserve it from injury or damp. In the better quality Turkish bows, this outer coating of bark or leather is often lacquered in brilliant colours and decorated with gold leaf. The thin lath of wood which forms the core of the bow confers no strength on it; it merely acts as the nucleus round which the horn and sinew are glued.

The bowstring is made from skeins of twisted silk, knotted at each end to receive the nocks of the bow's arms.

The bow was strung in such a manner that its concave form in the unstrung state became convex when ready for action. It thus follows the same combination of tension and compression as occurs in a modern built up gun. A good deal of muscular effort is required to string the Turkish bow and this is supplied by a combination of leg and manual power. Being short and stiff, this bow is extremely difficult to bend without mechanical assistance, so great care must be exercised during this trial of strength not to twist or warp the arms of the bow as this would damage it beyond repair. It was part of the Turkish soldier's training to effect this stringing by leg and hand efficiently. The Turk always wore a thin horn groove on the thumb when firing this weapon.

The range of the Turkish bow in the hands of a well-trained archer varies between 600 and 800 yards.

These oriental bows being short and light were allotted to horse-men as well as to foot-soldiers. Hence the expression 'Parthian

35

shot' which originated from the practice of the mounted man advancing to fire his bow and then wheeling around and galloping away.

The last of the personal weapons of this period was the *arbalasta* or cross-bow. Although it may be classed as an engine of war, it takes an intermediate place between the early military machines

From an illuminated Turkish MS. in the Sloane Collection, B.M., dated 1621, No. 5258. These reproductions plainly show how small was the size of the bow formerly used in warfare by Turkish soldiers.

Fig. 6.—Turkish cavalrymen with their bows.

and the primitive firearm; incidently, its belated appearance betokened a delayed departure. In certain European countries, notably Germany and Holland, it survives in a modern bullet-discharging form for sporting purposes where silence is essential, as for successful wildfowling. Another modern use is in game reserves where it is employed to inject dope into animals so that they may be secured without harm when their transportation is being arranged. It was extensively used in moving wild life during the construction of the Kariba dam. Even as late as 1965, the Soviet government placed an order for cross-bows with the firm of Jack Yeoman of Clerkenwell for firing hypodermic darts to render wild livestock innocuous.

Vegetius in his treatise on the military art dedicated to Valentinian II about A.D. 385 alludes to the cross-bow as being a weapon assigned to lightly armed troops. Unfortunately, he omits all description but the passage *Erant tragularii qui ad manuballistae vel arcuballistae dirigebant sagittas* admits of no doubt as to what is meant. Again, two Roman bas-reliefs of a date prior to the 4th century, now in the museum at Puy, France, present, according to Victor Gay,[1] all the characteristics of a primitive cross-bow. After these allusions darkness descends upon the scene and for the next five or six centuries no suggestion, either in art or writing, is forthcoming about this weapon. Perhaps it fell into disuse during the decline of the Eastern Empire, but whatever the reason (it may have been frowned on by other nations owing to its somewhat cumbrous nature) the cross-bow appears to have remained in abeyance during the Dark Ages.

By the 10th century, however, it was again being used. When Senlis was attacked by King Louis[2] in A.D. 947 the cross-bowmen of the city saved the day and compelled the king to raise the siege; and in the attack on Verdun by Lothair[3] in A.D. 985 cross-bowmen were employed. Although no pictorial representation of this mechanical contrivance appears in the Bayeux tapestry, it is known that the Normans brought it with them to England. Both Guy, Bishop of Amiens, and William of Poitou, chaplain and biographer of William the Conqueror, record its use at the battle of Hastings. It is also stated that William Rufus was accidently killed in the New Forest by a bolt discharged from a cross-bow by Sir William Tyrrel. The Norman and earlier Angevin kings employed crossbowmen in their armies till its use became dormant as a result of a papal bull issued by Innocent III in A.D. 1193. This denounced

[1] *Archaeological glossary of the Middle Ages and the Renaissance* by Victor Gay. Paris. 1887.
[2] Louis IV of France (A.D. 936–954).
[3] King Lothair of France (A.D. 955–986).

37

the use of such a barbarous weapon among themselves by the nations of Christendom, though the infidel was exempt from this charitable dispensation.

Richard I held the cross-bow in great esteem and encouraged its use, not only among his own troops but in other armed forces in Europe. His enthusiasm popularised the weapon to a large extent and helped to overcome the prejudice against it caused by Innocent's bull. This assisted its re-introduction as a common arm in war. Richard I relied on the cross-bow in his crusade to the Holy Land and in his wars against France. Brompton,[1] writing of him, said 'Truly, this kind of shooting, already laid aside, which is called cross-bow shooting, was revived by him, when he became so skilful in its management that he killed many people with his own hand'. It was also the case of the biter bit. Richard fell a victim to his own policy for as William le Bruton[2] says 'Thus perished by the cross-bow, which the English account dishonourable, King Richard who first introduced the cross-bow into France'.

John and Henry III employed considerable numbers of mercenary cross-bowmen in their armies, both mounted and foot, but after the death of the latter the English preference for the long bow asserted itself, not only on account of its utility as a weapon but also for its tactical advantages. Englishmen had never really taken the cross-bow to their hearts and when the properties of the long bow were realised, the former declined in public favour. On the continent, the Genoese were the great protagonists of the crossbow and 6,000 of them were employed by the French at Crécy. Owing to weather conditions, however, their weapons failed on service and the English archers carried the day. In spite of this, the French adopted this arm and abandoned the use of the long bow; but the nation which lavished the greatest amount of ingenuity upon its improvement was the German who continued to use it after others had discontinued its employment. Despite its power, it was slow in action compared with the long bow and the latter in the hands of powerful well-trained men was the more telling weapon.

[1] John Brompton, monk of Jervaulx Abbey. Abbot in 1437. His chronicles record events between A.D. 588 and A.D. 1198.

[2] William le Bruton, Bishop of Tours. French chronicler. Born about 1170, died 1230.

In European armies, cross-bows as military weapons were in common use from about A.D. 1200 to A.D. 1470 but with English forces mercenary cross-bowmen were only employed till about A.D. 1300. During this period those armed with this weapon were regarded as a *corps d'élite* and were given pride of place in the battles of the day; and in the later stages of its use the cross-bow became so ornate and costly that in Spain cross-bowmen were

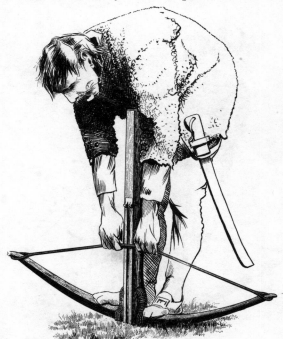

Fig. 7.—The primitive cross-bow.

granted the rank of knight, those of the mounted variety being more and more employed as a species of household troops. Thereafter, although by no means dispensed with, especially in siege operations, their numbers dwindled considerably. However, the end was in sight and between A.D. 1522 and A.D. 1525 the cross-bow as a weapon in open warfare was abandoned: ten years later it had become virtually obsolete for military purposes. The military cross-bow of the 15th century was a formidable implement. Those with a thick steel bow had an extreme range of some 380 yards and a point blank danger zone of about 65 yards. Two every-day expressions from the cross-bow era have survived the inter-vening centuries. We still say 'He has shot his last bolt' when we refer to a man at the end of his tether and speak about a sudden happening as a 'bolt from the blue'.

Fig. 8.—The improved primitive cross-bow with a stirrup.

The missile discharged from the cross-bow, usually named a *bolt*, was also called *quarrel, carreau, vireton, garro* and *garrock*. It was an iron dart about 2½ oz. in weight having a quadrangular head ending in a pyramidal point, winged with iron vanes or brass feathers for stability. *Quarrel* and *carreau*, deriving from *quadrus* (a square) refer to its shape of head, while *vireton* from *virer* (to twist) relates to the rotational motion imparted by the vanes or feathers. The derivation of *garrock* and *garro*, obviously variations of the same word, seems to have become lost. Primitive cannon fired a similar but heavier projectile.

The original cross-bow had its bow formed of one piece of

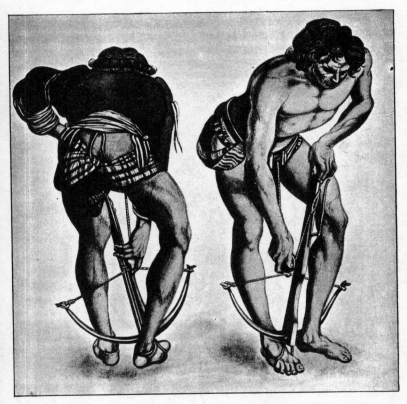

Fig. 9.—Cross-bowmen using the cord and pulley to bend their bows.

tough wood such as yew or ash. It was bent by drawing its string to the catch of the lock by the hands alone. It had no stirrup and the feet were pressed against the centre of the bow on the ground to obtain the requisite arming leverage. Anna Comnena,[1] daugh-

---

[1] Princess Anna Comnena. Born 1083, died 1148. Wrote the *Alexiad* in fifteen books.

ter of the Emperor Alexis I gives a good description of this primitive weapon in her writings. Afterwards, an iron stirrup was fitted
as a housing for the foot in order to expedite loading. A further
improvement was the substitution of a composite for a wooden
bow, to be followed during the middle of the 14th century by a
bow of steel. Between A.D. 1215 and 1300 various ingenious contrivances were devised to assist loading and increase range by a

Fig. 10.—Cross-bowman using a belt-claw to arm his bow.

greater compression of the bow. These were the cord and pulley;
the claw and belt; the screw and handle; the goat's foot lever; the
windlass, wheel and ratchet: the most important of these being
the last three. The goat's foot lever, so called from its supposed
resemblance to the hind foot of a goat, consisted of two pieces
hinged together. The smaller of these ended in catches which
grasped the bowstring on either side of the stock while the ends
of the larger portion to which was attached the lever handle, engaged lugs on either side of the frame. To charge the bow, the

lever handle was drawn back and the small forks which held the bowstring followed it until the catch of the lock was reached when the string was caught and retained. The loading apparatus could then be removed. This type was used chiefly with the smaller cross-bows carried by light horsemen. The windlass consisted of a system of pulleys and cords, one end of which was attached to the butt-end of the stock while the other was hooked to the bowstring. The cords passed over the end of the cross-bow and when actuated

Fig. 11.—Cross-bowmen using the windlass and goat's foot lever to arm their bows.

by the windlass pulled back the string till it engaged the catch. After loading, the tackle was removed and hung on the archer's belt. This particular loading accessory was only appropriate to the foot-soldier. The wheel and ratchet known as the *cranequin* was formed by a toothed wheel enclosed in a case engaging a toothed rod with a hooked end. When the wheel was turned by means of the handle the rod advanced and gripped the bowstring; when reversed, it drew back the string till it was held by the catch. A stout loop of cord fixed this apparatus firmly to the stock of the cross-bow. This was a powerful compact piece of mechanism eminently suitable for the heavier type of cross-bow used by mounted men and by those defending fortified places. Such soldiers were therefore sometimes termed *cranequiniers*. Lastly, there was the *arbalète à cric*. This was a later pattern with a stronger steel bow actuated by a more powerful windlass system built up of a double set of pulleys and cordage.

Fig. 12.—Cross-bowmen in action. From Froissart's *Chronicles*.

Thus all types of cross-bow consisted essentially of a wooden, composite or steel bow mounted on a frame or stock housing a lock and grooved to take a sliding block. The frame, except in the original pattern, was fitted at the fore-end with an iron stirrup to accommodate the foot during preparation for action. A bowstring connected the ends of the bow to the block which could either be drawn back by hand or a lever, or be wound back by some mechanical means until it was held by the catch of the lock operated by a trigger, thus placing the bow in a state of compression and arming the weapon. Loading was accomplished by placing the bolt in the groove in front of the block and discharge was effected by manipulating the trigger. This action allowed the lock to relinquish the string and the bow on re-assertion tautening the former with considerable force, projected the missile.

CHAPTER II

THE DEVELOPMENT OF ARMOUR

Having outlined the development of personal weapons and studied the means whereby man was able to kill his oponent, the methods of defence must now be examined. The first lesson in safety learned by prehistoric man was the art of taking cover, an instinct shared by all living creatures. Crouching behind a boulder or tree became second nature to him. This action, however, was passive in that it prevented room for manoeuvre and curtailed initiative—the two essentials for success in combat. Thus in due course active defence was developed. This took the form of a shield which afforded mobility to the bearer and widened his opportunities. This rather obvious piece of equipment has, in various shapes and sizes, been used all the world over from time immemorial. The earliest type was made of wood or wickerwork covered with raw hide, the shield of the Zulu warrior being a modern example of this kind of construction. The Bronze Age ushered in the bronze shield as early as 1000 B.C. The original patterns, usually circular in shape and about two feet in diameter, were fashioned with annular ridges round a circular boss and fitted with a grip-handle riveted to the back. The bronze face was strengthened by an underlay of raw hide impregnated with molten wax. This design was moderately proof against bronze weapons.

The shield employed by the early Egyptian soldiers was made of the usual wood or wickerwork covered by bull's hide, hair outwards. It was re-inforced by one or more rings of metal and studded with nails. It was three feet long and eighteen inches wide. A thong, by which it could be suspended from a man's shoulder when not required for use, was attached to the inside. The handle was placed so that the warrior could pass his arm through it and grasp his spear. As an alternative, the Egyptian soldier used a *pavoise*, a large shield stretching from his shoulder to the ground. The Ethiopians carried a shield similar to that of the Egyptians but the Persians preferred a shield of strongly compacted cane. The shield of the Roman legionary introduced at the time of Constantine was a hollow semi-cylinder of convex hexagonal shape rounded off at the corners measuring four feet in length and two and a half feet in breadth. Constructed of wood it was held together by small iron plates and covered by a broad piece of linen on which was fixed a covering of animal hide. It had a central boss. The German warrior carried a large shield usually adorned in brilliant colours though some were painted black. To discard a shield in battle was considered to be a heinous offence in Teutonic eyes.

The shield, also known as the buckler, target, targe or roundel, was an important article in Saxon military equipment. The Saxon warrior considered it to be indispensable in battle. It was circular in shape and made of linden wood. The face of the shield carried a protective covering of leather, the whole being strengthened by an iron boss—the umbo— projecting from the centre and covering a hole in the wood into which the left hand could be thrust to grasp the handle which stretched across the concavity. The convex front of the shield was often painted in some colourful design and in certain cases it was further embellished with metal studs. A strap was fastened inside whereby the shield could be slung round the neck or upon the back when not in use.

The Normans, being essentially a nation of horsemen, adopted the kite-shaped shield which gave them maximum protection with minimum interference. In action, it was held up close to the eyes with the left hand so that the broad upper part afforded protection to the greater portion of the body while the tapering end covered the left thigh. On the concave inner face was a hollow near the top supposed to be of service when the shield was slung on the back. Lower down were two hollow grooves parallel to each other, and these, covered with small straps, afforded a double handle for the left hand and arm. By the end of the 12th century, this kite-shaped shield underwent an alteration. The length was curtailed and the top made straight. These modifications transformed it into a 'heater-shaped' type, i.e. the kind of shield portrayed in heraldic drawings, and in this converted form it remained in use till the advent of firearms.

European warriors at first shunned all forms of protective covering save the shield. They considered any other kind of defence effeminate and unworthy of their dignity. On the other hand, the climate of southern Asia combined with its luxurious manner of life tended to sap the energy of its soldiers and undermine their fighting qualities. Therefore, to fight on equal terms with their adversaries they had perforce to adopt some additional means of

Fig. 13.—A Norman knight with archers armed with the long bow.

protection. Armour, thus, originated in the East and spread in due course to the West. So, in addition to the shield, armour made a general appearance at an early date. Originally composed of an animal's skin draped over the vital parts of the body, armour developed into a leather cuirass which in time was replaced by a metal breastplate. Helmets, too, were worn which ranged in style

48

from the skin cap to the iron head-piece. Leg coverings followed which eventually evolved into greaves; and gauntlets appeared to protect the hands and forearms.

It would be quite impossible to describe in detail the development of armour because of its wide distribution, nor would a survey of the western variety prove much more feasible. All that can be attempted is a short essay on the English types, remembering that armour like any other worldwide product followed a well-established pattern.

Soon after the disappearance of the Roman legionary, the character of armour changed. The leather jacket covered with metal plates gave way in the 5th century to a rudimentary form of chain mail. In the 6th and 7th centuries, the Franks and Lombards wore shirts of mail and some kind of helmet.

Since the study of armour is not without its difficulties, it is proposed to define certain items and describe the articles they represent for the benefit of those who may not be too familiar with the subject.

Habergeon. A coat of mail without sleeves; shorter than the hauberk.

Hauberk. Latterly a coat of mail, the word being derived from the German *Halsberge.* The small pattern, which was afterwards affected by squires and local magnates, was in the 8th century worn by all knights. It was a kind of jacket covered in scales which reached to the hips having loose sleeves ending just short of the elbow. The large hauberk on the other hand was tailored like a smock or frock. It had a *camail* or hood and originally reached to the knees and the elbows. Afterwards it was extended to become rather like a pair of modern combinations. Before the use of chain mail became standard, this garment was made in several ways. There was the ringed hauberk consisting of a rough leather foundation on to which were sewn adjacent metal rings. There was the *jazeran* or large hauberk covered with overlapping plates of bronze or iron. There was the *macled* type covered with small lozenge-shaped metal plates; and, lastly, there was the trellised coat made of leather or hide over which leathern thongs were interwoven, each interstice being strengthened by a riveted nail-head. When chain mail finally superseded the earlier rings and plates, the hauberk was composed entirely of iron mail without any lining or right and wrong sides. It thus

1. Specimen of the ringed coat (*Beringt*), composed of flat rings sewed side by side on quilted linen or leather.

    This kind of coat is very difficult, if not impossible, to distinguish from the macled coat, in the illuminations of different manuscripts. (See plate No. 4.)

2. Specimen of *rustred* coat (*Bekettet*). Here the flat rings are oval, and overlap each other half way.

    This sort of coat, in which the rings do not really interlace, is represented in illuminations as actual chain armour.

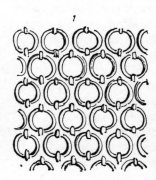

3. Specimen of *macled* coat (*Beschildet*). This is composed of small lozenge-shaped plates of metal, sewed on a foundation of cloth or leather, and sometimes overlapping each other half way.

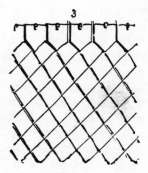

Fig. 14.—Specimens of ringed and macled coats.

formed a complete suit of flexible iron which could be donned like a shirt. Each ring was riveted piece by piece and the whole garment could be either of single or double mail. The arms were extended to cover the hands with a kind of pouch

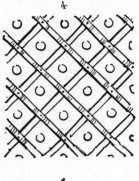

4. Specimen of trellised coat (*Gegittert* and also *Benagelt*). This coat is made both of quilted linen and skin, strengthened with straps of thick leather, placed trellis-wise; each square is armed with a riveted nail-head. It is difficult, in the illuminations on manuscripts, to distinguish the trellised from the ringed coat.

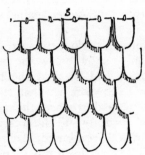

5. Specimen of scaled or imbricated coat (*Geschuppt*). It is also called *jazeran* and *korazin*. The armour consists of scales of metal sewed by rows, so as to overlap each other, on quilted linen or on leather.

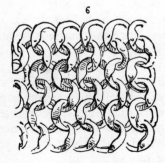

6. Specimen of coat of mail in riveted rings, called *grains d'orge* (*Genietetes Ketten* or *Maschengewebe*). Being entirely formed of metal rings, the coat of mail has neither wrong side nor lining.

Fig. 15.—A trellised coat, a jazeran and a coat of chain mail.

at the ends. These pouches were not gloved to accommodate individual fingers.

Gambeson. A thick padded garment without sleeves, stuffed with wool and quilted in vertical lines, worn under the hauberk. Later on, the lower edge was given a scalloped and fringed border. When the *cyclas* was introduced, it was worn over the gambeson.

Haqueton. A stuffed padded garment somewhat similar to the gambeson but less ornate. It was also worn under the hauberk.

Jupon. A light fitting sleeveless tunic.

Brigantine. A rather fancy garment used more for social purposes than for battle. The jacket itself was often made of velvet or of some other decorative material lined with linen. On the underside were riveted small plates of metal somewhat after the style of a macled coat so that its armoured portion was next to the body. All that was visible were small rivet heads. This was in reality the forerunner of the modern bullet-proof waistcoat as its object was to protect its wearer against sword or dagger thrusts.

Surcoat. Towards the end of the Norman period, the skirt of the tunic worn under armour began to show below the hem of the hauberk and by A.D. 1190 it had reached the knees. Fashions changed no less quickly 800 years ago than they do today and before long the tunic had reached the ankles. Suddenly, the situation changed abruptly and the wearing of the tunic under the chain mail was discontinued, leaving the latter to rest on the gambeson. The tunic itself was then worn over the armour like a linen overcoat. This garment, which was sleeveless, now became known as a surcoat. It was split up the back and front for convenience and was lengthened to reach down to the heels.

Ailettes. These were introduced in the latter part of the 13th century. Sometimes they were placed at the back of the arm, sometimes on the upper side of the arm and sometimes resting on the shoulders. They were made either of leather or metal and were of all shapes and sizes. It is uncertain whether their use was purely ornamental and intended for some heraldic device or defensive against sword cuts.

Genouillières. These knee-protecting pads were either of *cuir-boulli*, bronze or steel.

Greaves. These superseded thongs of leather wound round the leg for protective purposes. Originally made of leather they were afterwards fashioned of chain mail and finally of steel plate. They safeguarded the front of the leg, especially the shin bone, from injury. They performed the same function as the modern cricket pad.

Soleret. This was a steel shoe. Eventually the soleret and greave combined to form the steel jackboot.

Gauntlet. After the disappearance of the 'pouch' for the protection of the soldier's hand, the gauntlet took its place at the end of the 13th century. The first proper gauntlet had separate 'fingers' and was covered with overlapping scales. The back of the hand was concealed by a plate of leather or metal. The mitten, a kind of gauntlet in which the 'fingers' were not separated, had steel plates positioned to conform to the principal movements of the hand. It appeared in the 15th century. By the end of the latter century, the articulated gauntlet came into fashion.

Cyclas. This was a sleeveless tunic or surcoat made of linen, silk or some other suitable material. It reached the calves of the legs at the back but was shortened in front for convenience when mounted so that the under garments would not hamper the limbs.

There were quite a number of different head-pieces worn with armour, though four of them—the *salade*, the *morion*, the *armet* and the *burgonet*—did not come into existence until after the introduction of firearms.

The main types with which this survey is concerned are:

Casque. Only two kinds were known to exist. The horned pattern attributed to the early Scandinavians and Britons, and the conical type worn by the Assyrians, the Avars, the Germanic tribes, the Gauls and the Normans. These helmets were just iron hats.

Pot-de-fer. An iron skull-cap.

Heaume. This first appeared about the end of the 12th century. It was either crested or uncrested and developed from the conical casque which by then had acquired a nasal. Its evolution was gradual. Ear-flaps added to the casque became so enlarged that they absorbed the nasal and became a single piece of metal, short at the back and slitted in front for purposes of

120. Burgonet, splendid Italian work, in beaten iron, of the sixteenth century. In the Imperial Arsenal of Vienna, formerly in the Castle of Laxemburg. It is the finest specimen that exists of this sort, and has been satisfactorily photographed at the Industrial Museum of Vienna.

Fig. 16.—A burgonet.

vision. It was worn over a metal hood or *coif-de-mailles* and later over a hauberk. These in turn covered a pot-de-fer resting on the cranium. These additional head coverings were thought to confer extra protection to the head in battle but they suffered from the disadvantage of transmitting a blow on the heaume directly on to the skull of the wearer so that although an open wound might be avoided there was a distinct possibility of incurring a 'black-out' from concussion. To obviate this, the *pot-heaume* was designed, to keep the head from contact with the helmet. This type in one form or another survived for several centuries.

Basinet. This type of metal head-dress appeared in a number of guises. Some had vizors, some had not; some had brims, others had not. Certain patterns were used in conjunction with gorgets, and when the vizor was lowered they gave almost complete protection to the face. These numerous forms no doubt betokened a desperate search for suitable methods of safeguarding the head, face and neck. They changed their shape to nullify the effects of weapons which over the years had been improved in deadliness.

Among the early Saxons in England none but the leaders wore armour, and even by the time they met the Norman host under William the Conqueror at Senlac, the rank and file of the Saxon army had to be content with a thick leather coat girded in at the waist. The *byrnie* or hauberk of the Saxon notables consisted of a leather garment on to which were sewn metal rings or scales. It is a moot point whether chain mail had penetrated into England at that time. Some have ascribed its invention to the Gauls while others have affirmed that it hailed from the East. It was certainly in use on the continent before the 9th century. The Saxon helmet was constructed of a framework of thin iron or bronze bands strengthened by a covering of leather. One passed round the head just above the ears. From this as a foundation, two other bands arose, one stretching from the forehead to the back of the skull the other from side to side. Towards the end of the 10th century the band rising from the forehead was lengthened to include a nasal for protecting the face from a sword cut, and this practice became universal in the following century. Saxons also wore a metal Phrygian cap which was usually crested.

The period between the Norman conquest and A.D. 1180 was one of transition brought about by new or improved weapons which threatened the efficacy of existing armour. This was the age-old struggle between the weapon and its antidote, the rivalry between attack and defence, the effort to obtain mastery in the field which has been a feature of warfare since man first improved his club. The most important weapon which now began to make its appearance was the long bow, first used by the English at the

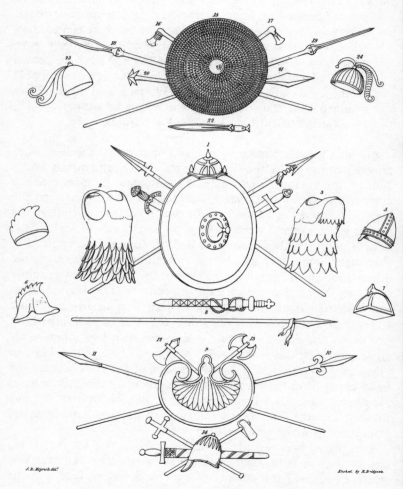

Fig. 17.—British, Saxon and Danish armour.

battle of the Standard on 22nd August A.D. 1138. The armour of
the Normans consisted of the hauberk, conical casque and shield,
and their weapons were the lance, javelin, battle-axe, sword, mace
and bow. They had an additional piece attached to the hauberk
called a pectoral, which consisted of a square or oblong bit of
material worn on the chest. It acted as a reinforcement for the

1. German equipment of the eleventh century, from the statue of one
   of the founders of the Cathedral of Naumburg. The casque is similar
   to that in the Codex Aureus of Saint Gall. Strangely enough, the
   right leg is without armour. A beard is seen on the chin.
2. German warrior of the eleventh century, in a hauberk with long
   sleeves, hood, and breeches and leggings in mail. From the
   Jeremias Apocalypsis, in the library at Darmstadt.

Fig. 18.—German warriors of the 11th century.

neck and throat and covered the slit through which the head was passed when donning the hauberk.

The next important period was that of chain mail and its predominance over earlier forms of armour justifies this appellation

Fig. 19.—Richard I of England in chain mail and pot-heaume.

and differentiates it from the previous period. During the reigns of Richard I, John and Henry III, the heaume was developed, chain mail for hauberks was devised and the surcoat appeared. Personal arms remained much the same except that the cross-bow made a fitful appearance, the long bow improved and the military pick came into existence. The latter was a weapon designed for piercing chain mail. Slingers were also in evidence.

The next period, stretching from A.D. 1250 to 1325, saw chain mail reinforced and becoming a more complete covering for the person. The *coif-de-mailles* was continuous with the hauberk and

Fig. 20.—A spearman and a slinger.

was worn over a *pot-de-fer*. The mail *chausses* covering the feet and legs had, in the case of a knight, prick spurs fastened over them by straps. The sleeveless surcoat, split up the front to the waist was often of rich material and fringed. *Genouillières* were introduced to give protection to the knees. Gauntlets, continuous with the chain mail sleeves, were not divided for the fingers.

Towards the end of the 13th century banded mail made its appearance and remained in almost universal use for a hundred years. Its adoption coincided with the increased employment of the long bow. The heaume now became more pronounced in shape and *ailettes* became the fashion. New weapons introduced into England during this period were the *estoc* and the *anelace*. The former, a stabbing sword, possessed a long narrow blade for thrusting, while the latter was a broad-bladed dagger with a double edge. The cross-bowmen were protected by a *haqueton* and a *basinet* provided with a collarette of iron.

The decline of chain mail in popularity which now began to be evident may be ascribed to the following causes. The coats of mail used during the earlier crusades had been tough enough to resist Saracen arrows but they proved powerless to keep out those from the English long bow. They were also not proof against the bolts of the cross-bow. Chain mail was often fractured or torn by a lance thrust and it proved ineffectual against a mace or battle-axe because, although the mail might remain undamaged, the body underneath might be seriously hurt by the blow. When plate armour was introduced, the defence for a short time became a match for the attack. This phase lasted till the firearm appeared, when the scales tipped again in favour of the latter.

Once chain mail came under suspicion, a completely new type of armour was evolved. This consisted of a number of thickly padded loose garments combined with a judicious mixture of chain and plate. The phase was known as the cyclas period and lasted ten years during which the *cyclas* or *cyclatoun* was adopted. This garment was worn with the gambeson, the hauberk of banded mail, the haqueton and a breastplate with one or two other pieces of plate in special positions. Basinets, with or without vizors, with *camail* or a *coif-de-mailles* over a *pot-de-fer* were the head coverings preferred. This period in turn was followed by others of short duration, each striving to defeat the attack by means of a better defence. The struggle between the two dragged on, the advantages sometimes with the defence, at others with the attack. This 'tug-of-war' lasted till plate armour was ushered in as the final answer to the contest between weapons and armour.

Plate armour is beyond the scope of this book. It was the

armourer's last throw on the wheel of fortune against the firearm but it failed. Although the bullet of the late 16th century had a poor velocity, it was sufficient to penetrate plate armour at short range because the steel of that period was not bullet proof except

Gothic armour of polished steel, of the fifteenth century, the casque, a kind of *heaume*, has a rounded crown, and hinged vizor; it is attributed to Frederick I., Count Palatine of the Rhine, who died in 1476.

Ambras Collection, Vienna.

A similar suit, in the same collection, is attributed to Frederick the Catholic.

This war harness, as is obvious at first sight, belongs to the middle of the fifteenth century, from the singular form of the tassets, the gauntlets, and the ends of the solerets, one of which is represented in full, by the side of the left leg. The casque already partakes of the character of the armet, and seems to be more modern than the rest of the armour.

Fig. 21.—A suit of plate armour; 15th century.

in such a thickness as to make the weight of a suit of armour unbearable. It should be appreciated that armour as an item of military equipment had become largely redundant by the close of Henry VIII's life. The reign of Elizabeth I ushered in the era of enriched armour. The suits produced, not only at Greenwich but in the great continental workshops, were ornate to a degree and vied with one another in richness and inlay. Ceasing to be of any value on the battlefield, armour became a matter of display for the tournament. It was the final paean which heralded its swansong. Wealthy nobles spent fabulous sums on exotic suits which served no useful purpose save to enhance the personal adornment of their wearers and add to the general pageantry of the tilt. By Stuart times armour had sunk to a purely sartorial level. Therefore, as the 17th century advanced the work of the armourer declined in importance. No doubt the realisation of its approaching doom was hateful to all concerned. For three centuries armour had been resisting the encroachment of the firearm, but the march of events proving overpowering, the bullet emerged the victor.

The final phase was the perennial story of man's resistance to change. Although Tennyson tells us that 'The old order changeth, yielding place to new', human inertia against adopting new techniques is very marked. It even took centuries before the firearm finally superseded the bow, for 250 years after the arrival of the handgun Montaigne could still lament its appearance. There was a halo of romance surrounding armour and all that it represented which made kings and nobles loth to abandon it. It was the last vestige of feudalism wherein the armed knight considered himself a being apart from the common foot-soldier, and it degenerated at last into an emblem of snobbery. But evolution cannot be turned aside and armour had to join other phantom equipments in the dustbins of history. Its fate in England was sealed by the martyrdom of Charles I, after which the famous Greenwich Armoury closed its doors for ever.

CHAPTER III

ENGINES OF WAR

War breaks out when two groups of people reach deadlock over a matter of vital importance. When differences of opinion appear, the first course open to the protagonists is to parley. Envoys are sent to talk matters over with their opposite numbers. Should such a meeting prove abortive, a series of notes are exchanged till one side or the other, losing patience, forwards an ultimatum. This is the last shot in the locker of the diplomat; no further step in settling the dispute is open to the parties and the stage for conflict is set. Reason having failed, force takes over. This is why war has been defined as the ultimate resource of policy. The tongue and pen having been overwhelmed in the rising torrent of discord, the the sword is left as the arbiter of fate.

The above is a short summary of events which normally precedes a declaration of war. In earlier times the steps were possibly not so clearly defined. 'Grab while you can' has often been a convenient motto for the tyrant who coveted his neighbour's property. In our own day the programme of events is apt to be more elaborate owing to the complexity of our way of life. Even within the last thirty years ultimatums have been discarded on several occasions in the opening gambits of hostilities.

The principles of war, as has been said, never alter, and certain axioms must be followed. Thus definite types of weapons have of necessity been perpetuated. The soldier must have his personal arms for in-fighting and for striking at a distance: the leader must have under his control contrivances to batter down resistance so that his army may reap the final fruits of victory. These must be able to offer both direct and indirect fire to enable him to achieve his object. In defence, too, the basic doctrines have remained constant. The British Tommy in World War I never said a truer word than when he called his 'tin hat' a 'basin hat' for it was nothing more than a modern version of the basinet of the early 14th century.

The following table gives the relationship between ancient and modern armaments and clarifies the association of the equivalent weapons of the Greeco-Roman world and our own:

Engines of War	*Modern Equivalent*
Catapulta	
Onager	
Trebuchet	Howitzer
Mangonel	
Balista	Gun
Arbalasta	
Arcubalista	
Springald	Machine gun
Springalle	
Cross-bow	

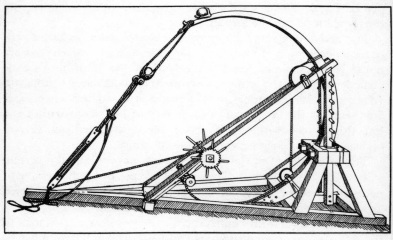

Fig. 22.—A springald.

A military machine is another term for an engine of war.

In order to depict the conditions under which sieges of the past were conducted the aspect of both the besieger and the besieged must be considered. The walled city probably existed prior to the introduction of engines of war but the latter undoubtedly hastened the provision and development of the fortified castle. The engines, known collectively as *balistariae* and *petrariae*, were originally of two kinds and bore a close relationship in action to that of their modern successors—the gun and the howitzer. Known as the *balista* and the *catapulta* respectively they each played a definite part in the symphony of bombardment. The former survived to the end of the mediaeval period but the latter owing to a decline in constructional skill was eventually superseded by the *trebuchet*, an invention ascribed to the French. There was a third mechanical weapon introduced much later. This was called the *arbalasta* or cross-bow which has been described in Chapter I. The authors on whom we depend for our knowledge about these machines are sometimes vague and often use loose phraseology when describing objects or events with which they were personally unfamiliar. Many of these writers took their facts from earlier historians with the result that a misleading nomenclature relating to engines of war has come down to us which bears little or no reference to their function.

Hero of Alexandria[1] and Philo of Byzantium[2] are the most trustworthy Greek authors who have left accounts of these machines. Both supply such accurate details that a very shrewd conception of the designs can be gathered from their works. Others[3] treat the subject less meticulously, but their writings are of value when studied in conjunction with those of Hero and Philo. Vitruvius[4] and Ammianus Marcellinus[5] are the chief Roman authorities and the former, obtaining his facts from the earlier Greeks, proves

---

[1] *Circa* 281–221 B.C. Invented the hydraulic clock.
[2] Engineer and mechanician. *Circa* 200–150 B.C.
[3]   (*a*) Athenaeus of Naucrates. 287–212 B.C.
    (*b*) Biton. *Circa* 250 B.C.
    (*c*) Apollodorus of Damascus. Architect and engineer. Contemporary with Hadrian and Trajan.
    (*d*) Diodorus Siculus. Historian. Born at Agyrium in Sicily. Contemporary with Julius and Augustus Caesar.
    (*e*) Procopius. Byzantine historian. Born at Caesarea, Palestine, *circa* A.D. 500. Died A.D. 565.
    (*f*) Polybius. Historian. Born at Megalopolis in Arcadia about 203 B.C. Died *circa* 128 B.C.
    (*g*) Josephus. Jewish historian. Born A.D. 37. Died *circa* A.D. 100.
[4] Vitruvius Pollio. Architect and military engineer. Born at Verona. Contemporary with Julius and Augustus Caesar.
[5] The last of the Roman historians. Born at Antioch. Died at Rome in A.D. 390.

that the Romans adopted siege engines from the Hellenes. Diodorus Siculus[1] mentions that military machines were first seen about 400 B.C. though it is now known that they existed many centuries earlier. He also says that when Dionysius of Syracuse[2] organised his great expedition against Carthage in 397 B.C. a genius among the assembled experts designed machines to cast stones and javelins. It was not, however, till the reign of Philip of Macedon[3] and that of his son Alexander the Great[4] that improvements in the technique and construction of these engines were seriously studied and their value in war recognised.

Vitruvius was primarily an architect though he could also claim to be an engineer, being the Inspector of Military Machines under Augustus. He has left the most careful descriptions of the *balista* and catapult. They are almost drawing-board blueprints and belong more to the world of the draughtsman than to that of the manufacturing craftsman. General designs were no doubt important but in the earlier part of the period under review these war machines were built on the spot as required by the military engineer of the army and his assistants, and each artisan held decided views based on his own experience. It was not till later when organisation and administration had improved that standard patterns of these machines began to take shape.

Vitruvius was not immune from error and one of his serious mistakes was to confuse the *balista* with the catapult. Although his description of both these forms of engine is excellent, he credits the former with hurling stones and the latter with discharging arrows or darts; whereas in reality the exact opposite took place: the *balista* fired the arrows and small pebbles and the catapults flung the stones. Such inaccuracies arise from the fact that only copies of the original writings of the old authors concerning engines of war exist. So it is perhaps only natural that incorrect drawings and descriptions arising from repeated transcriptions have filtered down to us. With few exceptions, all the historians mentioned give their own interpretation when in doubt about some technical point. This makes it difficult for the modern writer to present a balanced picture of the engines concerned.

[1] See 3 (*d*) above   [2] Tyrant of Syracuse. Born 430 B.C. Died 367 B.C.
[3] 360–336 B.C.   [4] 336–323 B.C.

One thing, however, does stand out clearly and that is that the engines made and used by the Romans after their conquest of Greece in 146 B.C. became in course of time inferior to the original types constructed by the Greek artificers. Their efficiency declined because the Romans neglected and finally lost the art of manufacturing certain vital parts; the most important of these were the skeins of sinew which alone gave life and power to all projectile-hurling machines. It is not now known of what tendons the sinews were composed, from what animal they were taken and in what manner they were prepared. Like the secret of Sheffield plate it has died with the craftsmen who perfected it. Sir Ralph Payne-Gallwey[1], who carried out many trials with replicas of ancient engines he had built, says that every kind of sinew, hair or rope which he tried either broke under the strain or lost its elasticity in a short space of time when subjected to great stress, thereby rendering constant renewal necessary if the serviceability of the models was to be maintained. He found skeins of hempen rope to be inferior in both strength and elasticity to those made from animal tissue. The arms of all military machines were known to be laminated, i.e. formed of several spars of wood interleaved with lengths of thick sinew fitted longitudinally and bound round with broad strips of raw hide which afterwards set as hard and light as a sheath of metal. But again the method of manufacture has been lost and the secret of constructing a light and flexible arm of sufficient strength for the catapult to bear the violent strain imposed upon it lies buried in the sands of time.

In addition to the generic terms, a host of fanciful names embellishes the writings of early military historians; names more suitable to opera-bouffe than to a serious discourse on warlike equipment. Examples are the *scorpion*, the *robinet*, the *mate-griffon*, the *bricolle*, the *bugle* or *bible*, the *mata-funda* and the *war-wolf*. All these designations, however, referred to dart or stone-throwing machines operated on a torsional or counter-weight principle, except the *mate-griffon* which was a wooden tower constructed in A.D. 1190 by Richard I in Sicily and named as a reproach to the *Griffones* (Greeks). The word *mate* appears. to have been derived from *donner eschec et mat*, a favourite court

---

[1] *Projectile-throwing engines of the Ancients.* Longmans, Green and Co., 1907.

game of those days. (The modern equivalent is *checkmate* in chess.) Richard had this tower dismantled in A.D. 1191, conveyed to the Holy Land and re-erected before the walls of Acre.

The *war-wolf* was a colossal trebuchet designed by Edward I for the siege of Stirling castle. It took five foremen and fifty carpenters much time and labour to build. Echoes of this come to us from a letter[1] written by Sir Walter de Bedewyne on 20th July 1304 to a friend:

'As for news, Stirling Castle was absolutely surrendered to the king without conditions this Monday, St. Margaret's Day, but the king wills it that none of his people enter the castle till it is struck with his *war-wolf* and that those within the castle defend themselves from the said *war-wolf* as best they can.'

It seems therefore that Edward was not a little chagrined by the capitulation of the castle's garrison before he had had an opportunity of demonstrating his secret weapon.

There were other pieces of apparatus used in the attack on fortified places besides *balistariae* and *petrariae*. These, of an engineer rather than of an artillery nature, were the ram (*aries*), the ram tortoise (*testudo arietaria*), the bore (*tenebra*), the mouse (*musculus*), the cat, the sow, the movable tower or belfry, scaling ladders and incendiary compositions. The latter are described in Chapter IV.

Although evidence concerning the introduction of projectile-throwing machines is lacking, there is a strong presumption that their cradle was ancient Greece. The first recorded mention of such engines places them about 1000 B.C. This occurs in the following passages in the Bible:

'And he made in Jerusalem engines invented by cunning men, to be on the towers and upon the bulwarks to shoot arrows and great stones withal.'[2]

and

'And he shall set engines of war against thy walls.'[3]

---

[1] Calendar of State Documents relating to Scotland.
[2] II Chronicles XXVI v. 15.   [3] Ezekiel XXVI v. 9.

XC

Fig. 23.—A form of extending scaling ladder.

Fig. 24.—A scaling ladder on wheels.

Thereafter Greek and Roman writers take up the tale.

After the eclipse of Greek hegemony in the Mediterranean, engines of war, as before stated, were adopted by the Romans who used them extensively in their armies. With the passing of Rome and the Western Empire they reflowered in Byzantium whence their tradition and employment spread to the civilised parts of Europe and the Middle East.

THE CATAPULT

Ammianus Marcellinus writes of the catapult as follows:

'In the middle of the ropes rises a wooden arm like a chariot pole . . . to the top of the arm hangs a sling . . . when battle is joined a round stone is set in the sling . . . four soldiers on each side of the engine wind the arm down till it is almost level with the ground . . . when the arm is set free it springs up and hurls forth from the sling the stone. This engine was formerly called the *scorpion* because it has its sting erect, but later ages have given it the name of *onager* or wild ass, for when such animals are chased they kick the stones behind them.'

The catapult will be described in simple terms, for the dimensions of the various parts given by Vitruvius are both complicated and confusing especially as he bases his design on the presumption that this engine discharges arrows instead of stones. His figures may be classified as ideal as it is doubtful whether many such machines built by military engineers of the time ever conformed to his specification. For example, he states in his opening paragraph:

'All the dimensions of the machine are given by the proposed length of the arrow it is intended to fire. The ninth part of this gives the size of the opening in the frame through which the twisted cords are stretched and wound as tightly as possible round the nuts above and below the cross-pieces which hold back the arm of the catapult.'

The frame or bed-plate, consisting of side pieces, cross-pieces, uprights and the roller for winding back the arm, was occasionally

Scale of 6 Feet.

Fig. 25.—A catapult known as an onager.

mounted on wheels for transport purposes; at other times the whole machine was erected *in situ*. The end of the revolving arm projected through a skein of twisted sinew to which was attached some form of ratchet enabling the skein to be put into a condition of initial torsion. There have been two types of arm in use. One, slender and pliant having a sling made of rope and leather attached: the other, thick and heavy, ending in a cup-shaped depression. The former was the earlier and more efficient form used by the

Fig. 26.—The pliant-armed catapult with sling.

Greeks and early Romans; it was lighter, more resilient recoiled with greater speed and, with the addition of the sling, increased the range by at least one third.

The ballistics were simple. The bigger the machine, the longer the arm, the wider the arc traced out and the greater the range. Theoretically, there was no limit to the size and therefore the range of the catapult, but practical considerations, such as the weight of the materials used and the strength of the arm, did restrict the overall magnitude. The projectile, which varied in weight according to the dimensions of the engine, was always composed of stone. To load and fire, the skein was torsioned to its limit, the sling was loaded and the arm racked back by the windlass attached to the roller till it was held by the retaining catch. On operating the quick release gear the catch disengaged and the arm flying forward opened the sling, and coming into sudden and violent contact with the cross-beam mounted on the two uprights, discharged its missile. Some of the more gigantic patterns could hurl a stone weighing 200 lb. The range was

Fig. 27.—The short-armed catapult with a cup-shaped depression at the end of the arm; used without a sling.

approximately 500 yards with a 50 lb. projectile. The finest machines were those designed and built by the Greeks, from whom the Romans borrowed the art; but with the decline of the Empire the cunning of her engineers fell away and subsequent engines suffered from defects in the arm and the skein and thus at a later date failed on service. In due course a more cumbrous type, in which the long slender pole was replaced by a short thick arm with a cup-shaped end, superseded the more elegant and efficient *scorpion*, but this change in design diminished its capabilities and militated against its use in action. The catapult, therefore, gradually faded from the scene of battle.

THE TREBUCHET

The *trebuchet* worked on the counter-weight principle; gravity, not twisted cords, being the prime mover. This machine was colossal compared to the catapult and much more powerful in its effects. It could hurl its 200 to 300 lb. projectile over a distance of 600 yards. Like the catapult, there was in theory no limit to the power of the *trebuchet*, its size and corresponding strength being conditioned only by the difficulties of manufacture and transport. Some of the larger examples had revolving arms fifty feet in length and counter-weights of ten tons. Slings were always part of its equipment. Missiles other than stones were used on occasions. Sometimes, dead horses were flung into beleaguered cities to cause pestilence; at others, rejected terms of negotiation nailed to the skulls of their unfortunate emissaries were returned by this machine. Incendiary compositions were also launched into walled towns as fire-raising agents.

An engine capable of flinging a stone weighing 12 cwt. accompanied the Genoese armament sent against Cyprus in A.D. 1376. Twenty-four engines captured by Louis IX of France at the evacuation of Damiella in A.D. 1249 afforded sufficient timber to build a stockade round his entire camp. A *trebuchet* used at the siege of Acre by the Crusaders in A.D. 1291 formed a load for a train of a hundred carts. A massive machine which had encumbered the tower of St. Paul at Orleans and was dismantled prior to the defence of the town against the English in A.D. 1428–29 furnished twenty-six cartloads of timber. Villard de Honne-Court, an engineer of the 13th century, describes a *trebuchet* which had a counter-weight container holding some fifty tons of sand.

One of the last occasions on which the *trebuchet*, already obsolescent, was employed successively is described by Guillet[1] in his *Life of Mahomet*. The author writes:

'At the siege of Rhodes in A.D. 1480 the Turks set up a battery of great cannon, but the Christians successfully opposed the cannon with a new invention. An engineer aided by the most skilled carpenters in the besieged town made an engine that cast pieces

[1] French historian 1625–1705.

75

Fig. 28.—The trebuchet.

of stone of a terrible size. The execution wrought by this engine prevented the enemy from pushing forward the work of their approaches, destroyed their breast-work, discovered their mines and filled with carnage the troops that came within range of it.'

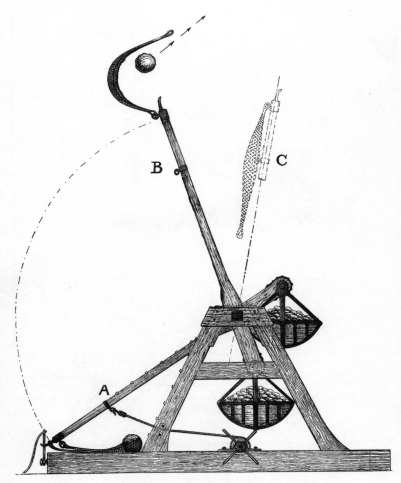

Fig. 29.—The trebuchet in action discharging its missile.

Fig. 30.—A trebuchet.

Fig. 31.—Various types of trebuchet.

It was of course no novelty that Guillet recorded but the resuscitation of a well-nigh forgotten weapon which the advancing claims of artillery had driven from the field. Probably the ultimate appearance of this machine in action was at the siege of Mexico by Cortes in A.D. 1511. Prescott in his *Conquest of Mexico* writes that when the Spaniards ran out of gun ammunition, a soldier with a flair for engineering undertook to make a *trebuchet* which would cause the town to surrender. A massive erection was therefore built but, the aspirant's theoretical knowledge evidently outstripping his practical ability, it was destroyed by the descent of its first missile.

The *trebuchet* was simpler in design than the catapult. It consisted of a bed-plate carrying two upright frames which housed the axle transfixing the revolving arm. One end of the arm carried the sling, the other the counter-weight. In addition, there was a windlass for winding down the arm to the firing position where it was held in place by a quick-release retaining catch. For loading, the arm was fully wound back. On release, the force of gravity acting on the counter-weight revolved the arm and discharged the missile.

THE BALISTA

Again, Vitruvius waxes lyrical over the *balista*, giving the most careful measurements for the different parts of the apparatus. Again, his account is far from clear as it is based entirely on the weapon hurling stones instead of projecting arrows which was its main purpose in action. This instrument is to our eyes extremely simple in comparison with modern machines and its simplicity demands a plain uncomplicated description.

The *balista* furnished direct fire in place of the high-angled rounds delivered by the catapult and the *trebuchet*. There were two types. One projected *quarrels* or bolts (iron darts feathered with brass) and the other small stone shot. They were employed in field as well as in siege warfare and their size depended on the nature of their employment. Smaller patterns were used extensively in the defence of battlements. The more powerful models could hurl a bolt weighing 5 or 6 lb. a distance of about 500 yards.

Fig. 32.—The *balista*.

Pub. 1st April 1767 by J. Hooper

The *balista* was in reality a huge cross-bow fixed to a stand. It consisted of a wooden pedestal carrying a movable top-carriage divided into three compartments, the two outer of which housed twisted skeins of fibrous material each containing a short lever. The central compartment supported the cradle which had a rack,

Fig. 33.—Another type of *balista*; sometimes known as an *arcubalista*.

a block and a winding gear. Ropes were attached to the block from the ends of the levers which were held in a state of torsion. There was, in addition, a quick-release gear to free the block. To load and fire, the block was windlassed back along the cradle so that the skeins became even more torsioned, thereby supplying the propulsive power. A bolt or small stone was then inserted in front of the block, aim taken and the retaining catch released. The block flying forward under the impetus of the torsioned skeins propelled the missile. As an example of its penetrative power Procopius[1] relates that during the siege of Rome by Vitiges, King of Italy, in A.D. 536 he saw a Gothic chieftain in armour pinned to a tree by a bolt discharged from a *balista*. A similarly discharged *quarrel* during the siege of Paris in A.D. 885 passed through the bodies of several soldiers.

THE RAM AND BORE

The ram used in siege warfare was of two kinds; the simple and the compound. The former was merely a large spar of timber carried on the arms and shoulders of men and actuated by their repeated charges. The latter consisted of a huge ironshod pole slung about its centre of gravity from a travelling framework usually mounted on wheels. The implement earned its name from the fancied resemblance its reinforced head bore to that of the male sheep. The compound pattern was more efficacious. As the heavy pole hung in a position of swinging equilibrium comparatively little effort was required to strike repeated blows of an increasing weight at the same point of impact. In this manner, breaches were made in the masonry of the besieged's walls. Mark Anthony in the Parthian war used a ram eighty feet long,[2] and Vitruvius records that these contrivances sometimes attained a length of 120 feet. In exceptional cases, the manning party numbered two shifts of a hundred men each so that continuous action could be maintained when required. Dr. John Desaguliers[3] demonstrated, in the annotations to his second lecture on experimental philosophy delivered in London in or about A.D. 1710, that the momentum of a battering ram 28 inches in diameter and 100 feet long with a cast-iron head weighing $1\frac{1}{2}$ tons—the whole weighing 18 tons—would, if moved by the united strength of

---

[1] See 3(*e*) above.   [2] Plutarch. *Circa* A.D. 66.
[3] John Theophilus Desaguliers (1685–1744). Born at Rochelle. Son of a Huguenote pastor. He studied at Christchurch, Oxford, and took holy orders. He lectured in London on optics and mechanics from 1710 onwards. Published fourteen works. His youngest son, Thomas, became a Lieut-General in the Royal Regiment of Artillery and was the first officer of that regiment to be elected a Fellow of the Royal Society. Born 1725. Died 1st March 1780.

Fig. 34.—The simple ram.

1,000 men, only equal that of a 36 lb. cast iron shot fired at point-blank range.

The bore was much smaller than the ram. It also had an armoured head. Its role was to sap through the walls at their base with a view to undermining foundations. When a sufficiently

Fig. 35.—The compound ram.

85

large penetration had been effected the aperture was widened to admit of the wall or tower being underpinned with planks and fired, causing the stonework to collapse.

The tortoise, mouse and cat were varying names for stoutly constructed pent-houses with sloping roofs covered with clay and raw hides. They were employed as a protection against fire and

Fig. 36.—The bore housed in a mouse.

injury for those working the ram and the bore and for the miners who 'fired the charges'. The tortoise normally housed the ram while the smaller mouse afforded cover for the bore. Sometimes, these devices were very elaborate; they were often mounted on wheels and strengthened by towers and guardhouses. They were then referred to as *chats-châteaux*. The terms 'cat' and 'sow' indicated that the soldiers within either waited for their prey with feline patience or lay like a litter safe from assault.

The ram is said to have been first employed by the Carthaginians at the siege of Cadiz. Having captured a fort the attackers set about its destruction. Since they lacked iron tools for their purpose, they took a heavy beam and raising it manually swung it to and fro against the wall to effect their objective. Subsequently,

Fig. 37.—The ram housed in a tortoise.

a Tyrian engineer—Pephrasmanos by name—improved the idea. He set up a pole and from it suspended a crossbeam like that of a balance. This he caused to be drawn backward and thrust forward till the violence of its blows finally overthrew the walls of Cadiz. Ciras, the Carthaginian, was the first to make a wooden platform on wheels upon which he constructed a pent-house with uprights and cross-pieces. In this he suspended a ram which he protected with ox-hides for the greater safety of the crew within. Since this contrivance was slow in action, he called it the ram tortoise. Afterwards, Polyidus, a Thessalonian, prepared a variety of simpler designs for Philip, son of Amytas, who was laying siege to Byzantium. His methods were continued by his pupils, Diades and Charias, who accompanied Alexander the Great on his campaigns.

This ram tortoise had a breadth of 48 feet, a height (less the gable) of 24 feet and the height of the gable from the platform to the summit 24 feet. The gable projected three feet above the middle of the roof. Above this was placed a small tower six feet wide and three stories high. The top story housed *scorpions* and catapults while in the lower was stored water against the risk of fire. In this erection the ram was placed on a platform of rollers covered with raw damp hides so that the men detailed to work the ram and fire the machines had ample protection from missiles and incendiary material. The bore was constructed in a similar manner though it was housed less ornately. The machine itself had a channel in the middle resting on uprights, 75 feet long and 18 inches high, on which was set a windlass cross-wise. At the front were two pulleys, one on either side, by which the beam shod with an iron head was moved along the channel. Under the beam in the channel itself were rollers fixed at frequent intervals to render the movement of the bore more rapid and powerful. Above the beam arches were placed along the channel to support the raw hides in which the apparatus was enveloped.

Movable towers in Greek days were often of great magnitude. Hero of Alexandria distinguishes three classes varying in height from 90 to 180 feet. The smallest had ten, the next fifteen and the largest twenty stories. They were all mounted on wheels. Some had balconies on the upper floors protected by hides. Diades in

Pub: 26.th Feb.y 1788 by S.Hooper.

N.C Goodnight sculpsit.

Fig. 38.—A movable tower.

89

his book gives the various dimensions and measurements of these gigantic towers with which it is not proposed to weary the reader. In later times, movable belfries became more restrained in size, seldom exceeding four stages. A drawbridge was usually housed in the top floor to help the besiegers to gain the parapet of the opposing bastion. These towers were used as covered approaches for the final assault. Scaling ladders, climbing machines and grappling hooks also assisted the attacking force to gain their objective.

SIEGE DEFENCES

So far we have dealt only with attack. How did defence fare under the conditions described? There was no special equipment for defensive purposes save boiling oil and molten lead for the heads of the assault party. In addition, the besieged could lob incendiary compositions on to the opposing camp, pour down fire on to the rams and movable towers, discharge arrows through embrasures and discomfort the enemy by firing stones and bolts from light *balistae* mounted on the ramparts. As Vitruvius truly says: 'Different tactics require different stratagems and there are no hard and fast rules for defence.' Stout hearts, determination and enterprise in the face of pestilence, starvation, fire and death were the only reliable qualities to sustain a beleaguered garrison. Surrender was out of the question since it spelt slavery or extermination for the men and concubinage for the women. War has ever been an unprofitable business.

Diognetus, an architect of Rhodes, became the city's engineer during the fourth century B.C. During his tenure of office, Callias, an architect from Aradus, lectured to the Rhodians about the possibility of erecting on their walls a great revolving crane which he claimed could seize any offensive engine of war as it approached the ramparts and lift it into the city. Thereupon, the Rhodians approving the project dismissed Diognetus and appointed Callias in his place. Meanwhile, King Demetrius declared war on Rhodes and brought with him Epimachus, a famous Athenian architect, who constructed a colossal siege engine 125 feet high, 60 feet broad and weighing, it is said, almost 175 tons.

It was so overlaid with goatskins and ox-hides that it could withstand the blow of a stone weighing three cwt. projected from a military machine. It was named the *City Taker*. When Callias was asked by the Rhodians to fashion an instrument to neutralise the effects of the City Taker he confessed his inability to do so. Diognetus, again restored to favour, eventually agreed to save his city provided he could keep the mammoth engine should he be able to capture it. Having obtained consent to his proposition, Diognetus made a breach in the wall where the machine was to

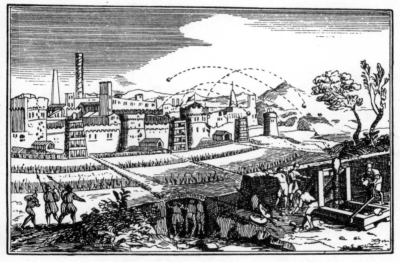

Fig. 39.—A fortified town under assault by catapults.

enter and ordered all and sundry to pour as much water, sewage and mud as possible along the path beyond the breach. This was accomplished overnight and when next morning the City Taker advanced to the attack it was engulfed in a morass and rendered powerless of movement. Demetrius, realising he had been tricked by Diognetus, raised the siege and sailed away. The City Taker was carried in triumph into Rhodes and set up in the market place.

When Apollonia in Illyria was besieged by Philip V of Macedon in 214 B.C. the attackers burrowed under the walls to obtain

Fig. 40.—A castle under siege.

entrance into the town unobserved. This manoeuvre was reported to the Apollonians by spies. Whereupon Trypho of Alexandria, the engineer in charge of defence, planned a series of counter-tunnels to emerge about 200 yards beyond the ramparts and in them hung a number of bronze vessels to act as sound-locators to detect hostile movement. Having ascertained the enemy's

Fig. 41.—A fortified town under siege by catapults and *balistae*.

underground line of advance, he filled cauldrons with boiling oil, pitch, sand and human dung brought to a fiery heat. During the night he pierced a number of openings into the hostile excavations and, flooding them with the contents of the 'hot-pots', killed all the troops working therein.

Finally, when Marseilles was attacked by the Romans in 49 B.C. the enemy excavated more than thirty tunnels, but the inhabitants being on their guard constructed a ditch deeper than the one in front of the ramparts so that all the hostile tunnels emerged into it. Inside the walls, however, where a ditch could not be made they dug a moat and filled it with water from wells and the

Fig. 42.—A fortress under assault.

harbour. Thus when a tunnel had its passage suddenly opened the rush of water threw down the props supporting the roof. The troops within, overwhelmed by the collapse of the tunnel and the flood of water, perished. The Romans also built a great mound against the walls and raised its height by laying felled trees on its summit. In retaliation, the citizens shot red-hot iron bars from their *balistae* and set fire to the earthwork. Lastly, a ram tortoise was brought up to demolish the wall, but the defenders let down a rope and caught the head of the ram. They then wound the rope round a drum using a windlass, and by keeping the ram elevated, prevented it from touching the wall. In the end they

Fig. 43.—The capture of a fortress.

destroyed the whole engine by incendiary missiles and stone shot from their *balistae*.

These examples must suffice to show the various ruses employed by the defence.

To give some idea of the number of war engines employed in sieges of the past, it may be mentioned that Livy records the capture of 120 large and 200 small catapults together with 33 great and 52 lesser *balistae* at the conquest of Carthage in 146 B.C. Abulfaragio[1] states that Richard I of England and Philip II of France employed 300 catapults and *balistae* at the siege of Acre in A.D. 1191.

Engines of war, like all other human inventions, could not resist the destroying hand of progress. The advent of gunpowder in the 13th century heralded their passing and as the power of artillery increased their usefulness decreased until at last they vanished for ever from the battlefield. With their departure war began to lose that pageantry which the Age of Chivalry had bestowed upon it.

[1] Arab historian. 1625–1705.

CHAPTER IV

INCENDIARY COMPOSITIONS

Incendiary compositions, like the rose-red city, are half as old as time, for fire was one of the first secrets wrested from nature by man. He soon realised its potentialities for good or evil, comfort for himself or anguish for his foes. Primitive man was quick to appreciate the horrifying qualities of arson, as fire, used in this way is one of the most destructive agents in the world, terrifying alike to humans and animals.

Incendiary compositions were an adjunct to ancient warfare as early as 1000 B.C. Tow and pitch formed the staple ingredients and fire-pots containing these substances were flung down on besieging troops from the walls of strongholds under attack. The mixtures were classified under various names such as Greek fire, sea fire, Saracen fire and more recently wildfire. The original Greek fire was composed of sulphur, bitumen, resin, naphtha and tow with the possible addition of turpentine, charcoal and salt-petre. It was employed as early as the fifth century before Christ. Such inflammable material was hurled from machines with great effect at the sieges of Syracuse and Rhodes in 413 and 304 B.C. respectively. Aeneas[1] describes the generation of violent fire by the use of pots filled with a mixture of pitch, sulphur, pine shavings and resin. He explains how this incendiary mixture, attached to large wooden drums fitted with iron hooks at each end, could be launched on to the decks of ships where they lodged, or on to movable towers of besieging troops. The resultant flames defied extinction by water, vinegar being the only quencher.

This type of combustible mixture had continued in use for over 1,000 years when suddenly in A.D. 673 the Mediterranean world was startled by an improved form of Greek fire invented by Kallenikos. This was either projected by syphons placed in the prows of vessels or thrown in pots and phials. Its formula, jeal-

---

[1] Aeneas Tacticus, *Polyorkitikon* xxxiii–xxxv (Born 360 B.C.). Quoted by Dr. J. R. Partington in his *History of Greek Fire and Gunpowder*.

ously guarded, was regarded as a Byzantine state secret which in the 12th century was said to have been only in the possession of Lampros, a descendant of Kallenikos. No doubt its composition remained strictly confidential and the emperor, whose troops and engines were often put at the disposal of his companions in war, reserved to himself the recipe of this mysterious 'fire' and sent it ready prepared to his allies, as the Americans do today with their atomic warheads to their N.A.T.O. partners. There was quite a parallel in this respect between the Byzantines and the Pentagon. It had always been assumed that the art of preparing Greek fire had been lost in the dusty archives of the past till a certain Dupré claimed to have re-discovered it and sold the patent to Louis XV in 1756. In reality, the secret had never been lost; it had simply fallen into disuse when artillery displaced military machines and drove it from the soldier's mind.

From all accounts Greek fire seems to have inspired a feeling of absolute terror in the hearts of its beholders, though why such a state of panic should have been induced is hard to understand save on the assumption that superstition played a major rôle in mediaeval life. This composition was thrown against the crusading hosts by a *trebuchet*, and the Sire de Joinville,[1] present during such an attack, writes in a most exaggerated style concerning it. He relates how, comparable in size to a barrel of verjuice,[2] it swept forward emitting an awe-inspiring flame. He likens the sound made by its passage to the reverberation of thunder, and its appearance to a flying dragon. The light it emitted was said to render the camp as bright as day. Such was the fear felt by the commanders of the army of St. Louis[3] that Gautier de Carel, a brave and experienced knight, proposed that when Greek fire was being projected, all should sink to their knees and pray to Almighty God for protection against this evil from which He alone could deliver them. This pious advice was adopted and practised, the king himself lifting up his hands in prayer saying 'Good Lord God preserve my people'.

---

[1] Jean, Sire de Joinville. Born 1221. Seneschal to the Count of Champagne and King of Navarre. Died July 11, 1319.

[2] A 13th century flavouring sauce made by expressing the juice of crab apples. It was used in England in succeeding centuries.

[3] Louis IX of France (1248–54).

One wonders what action this saintly monarch would have taken in a modern air raid, or with what hyperbole the old scribes would have pictured a present day thermonuclear rocket attack.

Incendiary compositions, in addition to being hurled in containers or projected from syphons, were attached to arrows, javelins and spears, a practice which had obtained for over 2,000 years.

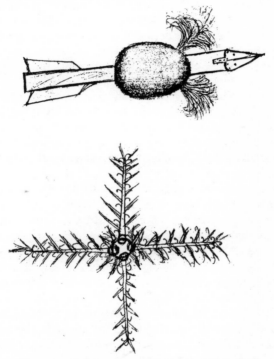

Fig. 44.—A fire-arrow and an incendiary ball.

In the 9th century B.C. Assyrian bas-reliefs show that these were employed at that time in siege operations, and Greek and Roman authors dilate upon this established custom during the various campaigns of antiquity. Virgil, Livy, Tacitus and Ammianus Marcellinus speak of fire-lances and fire-arrows which defied extinction by water. These missiles were of course terrifying on the early battlefield and their effect on draught animals must have been very marked. All over the ancient world fire was regarded as the ultimate deterrent. Such flying fire-carriers were in reality the first blue-print of the future incendiary shell fired from a gun, a conception not to be translated from the drawing board to the factory floor for well-nigh another two millennia.

Richarde Wrighte in his manuscript on guns and fireworks written in 1563 gives some crude but excellent drawings of fire-spears and fire-arrows well calculated to arouse alarm in the minds of the fearful. This shows that although the gun had been in existence for two centuries, commanders of armies were not averse to making use of man's earliest weapon, fire, because of its all-devouring effect.

Bitumen, naphtha and petroleum were well-known to many races in the ancient world and were used in their incendiary compositions as early as 500 B.C. Old writers are enthusiastic about these natural compounds when describing their fire-raising effects.

Here are half a dozen recipes for old-time incendiary mixtures:

(1) Grind 1 lb. of sandarach resin and 1 lb. of liquid gum ammoniac together in a pot and put it on a fire till the contents are melted. Then pour 4 lb. of Greek pitch over it to complete the composition.

(2) Mix petroleum, black petroleum, liquid pitch and oil of sulphur in a jar and bury it in horse dung for fifteen days. Then smear it over crows which can be flown against the enemy's tents.

(3) Powder together sulphur, resin, asphalt, sandarach, tartar, naval pitch and sheep's dung and dissolve them in petroleum. Put the resultant liquid in a jar and bury it for fifteen days in hot horse manure.

(4) An old recipe for making the earlier form of Greek fire was to take live sulphur, tartar, sarcocolle, pitch, boiled salt, petroleum oil and ordinary oil and boil them together. Then immerse tow in the mixture and set it on fire.

All these, unquenchable by water, could only be extinguished by strong vinegar, stale urine, sand or by felt soaked in vinegar and thoroughly dried.

(5) Work 4 lb. of lime, 4 lb. of sulphur and 2 lb. of benedict oil into a dough. Extinguishable only by oil.

(6) Mix well together 5 oz. of unslaked lime, 5 oz. of sulphur and $\frac{1}{2}$ oz. of benedict oil. Extinguishable only by milk.

Oil of sulphur was made by grinding 4 parts of sulphur in a mortar with 4 parts of oil of juniper and mixing them in a pot which was then placed on a gentle fire till distillation commenced.

Benedict oil (*oleum benedictum*), also called 'oil of bricks' (*oleum laterinum*) or 'oil of philosophers', was a red fetid empyreumatic oil distilled from pieces of brick soaked in olive, nut, hemp or linseed oil. It was described in chemistry textbooks up to the middle of the 19th century. It seems arguable whether it served any useful purpose in mediaeval firework manufacture.

Sandarach is a species of gum, and sarcocolle is a gum resin collected in Ethiopia.

Wildfire up to the 16th century consisted of:

Resin, rape oil, powdered glass, saltpetre, linseed oil, sublimate of mercury, camphor, verdigris, turpentine, sulphate of iron, arsenic, assafoetida, stone pitch, calcined calamite, spirits of wine, vinegar, verjuice, unslaked lime and red ochre.

These six recipes by no means exhausted the stock in trade of the alchemist.

It is interesting to note that the word *wildfire* is still used in the following context—'Rumour ran like wildfire through the camp'.

ROCKETS

The art of pyrotechny which governs the flight of powder rockets is of considerable antiquity. It was known and practised in the East, especially in China, in very early times and the Chinese are credited with being skilled firework makers many centuries ago. The original reason for pyrotechnic activity was spectacular, probably for displays at religious or other festivals. The effect on an uneducated peasantry must have been sensational and the awe which such scenes evoked contributed in no small measure to the idea of their employment for warlike purposes. It is uncertain, however, whether rockets were actually used in battle before the 14th century. The answer is probably in the negative as until gunpowder was discovered the firework would have been of little value in attack.

GAS

Although early man had no conception of gas as an offensive weapon, the idea is by no means new. It had raised its ugly head on several occasions before World War I. The first to advocate its use was the Emperor Leo VI (A.D. 886–911) who in his work on tactics proposed the use of asphyxiating fumes derived from wet quicklime which could be thrown in earthenware pots at the enemy. This charming character also suggested hurling venomous snakes within hostile lines.

The next occasion on which this obnoxious form of warfare was considered lies outside the time scope of this work but it has been included to show to what fantastic lengths the human mind can stretch. In the 16th century, Christopher of Hapsburg, a German artillery officer, put forward his plan which is, or was up till 1920, preserved in the great library at Strasburg. It consisted of attaching jars of poison gas to the backs of cats let loose on the battlefield. Christopher of Hapsburg submitted his proposal to the Council of One and Twenty at Strasburg. Needless to say, it was rejected on the ground of being impracticable, cats being independent creatures going where they will.

As Ecclesiastes truly states 'There is no new thing under the sun'.

CHAPTER V

EARLY EARTHWORKS AND FORTIFICATIONS

Man has ever sought shelter from his foes when the weight of circumstances was against him. Originally such protection was obtained by hiding in caves or behind some natural feature. When early tribesmen were liable to attack, these methods of taking cover were not always available in the immediate neighbourhood; some other means, therefore, had to be employed to guarantee safety. Earthworks were thus developed.

This system of achieving security was widely practised in Europe and North America but nowhere better exemplified than in Britain, which is rich in archaeological remains of this nature. These early British strongholds, carved out of the ground, consisted of strong natural positions strengthened by earthern ramparts divided by deep ditches. Many of them are of considerable age and far ante-date the Roman invasion. Quite a number are probably the work of Neolithic man. The early inhabitant of Britain, though the poet refers to him as 'an untutored savage', was no fool and had a shrewd sense of elementary tactics. He realised that any strong point to be safe must have a good all-round view—not to provide a field of fire, as his weapons had little or no range, but to afford a vantage point against surprise attack. He therefore constructed his defences on high ground. These hill camps were of two kinds, either those occupying the summit of a promontory which sloped steeply on all sides except where it joined the surrounding countryside, or those built on the crest of a hill which had to be encircled by ditches following the contours of the ground. In both cases, these man-made defences consisted of earthern banks the materials for which came from the ditches dug round the perimeter. An embankment and a fosse across the neck of land separating the promontory from its hinterland converted the height into a fortified enclosure, and the labour to construct this type of stronghold was obviously far less than that required to erect a hill fort. For the latter the work involved must have been enormous and the fact that so many of these early earthworks survive is a proof of the skill and engineering ability of our rude forefathers. One of the best examples in this country of a hill or contour fort is Maiden Castle in Dorset which was thoroughly surveyed by Sir Mortimer Wheeler in 1934–37.

This work crowns two eminences 434 and 444 feet high of an oval chalk hill one mile south-west of Dorchester. The central

Fig. 45.—Maiden Castle from the air.

plateau is ringed by numerous banks and ditches which vary from three on the north side to eight near the western entrance. It was first settled before 2000 B.C. by a Neolithic people who surrounded the eastern and lesser summit by a double ditch interrupted by causeways making an enclosure of about 12 acres. For some reason it was deserted by its original inhabitants but these were followed about 1900 B.C. by a group of the same culture who built a 1,790 foot barrow along the hill between the two ditches. Another flight then took place leaving the site empty for some 1,200 years. About 300 B.C. an Iron Age people re-occupied it and, fortifying the eastern summit with a ditch and a sheer-faced, timber revetted, earth-chalk rampart, enclosed another 16 acres with a single western and a double eastern entrance. Later, the ditch with a rubble rampart was extended round the western summit making in all a 46 acre enclosure safe from the danger of sudden attack. At the same time, the western entrance like the eastern was reconstructed, both having external works. In the middle of the 1st century B.C. the defences were re-modelled, the main rampart being heightened with inner revetments of masonry, and further outer lines of ramparts and ditches were added. Fifty years later the fortress seems to have been strengthened again. About A.D. 25 Belgic conquerors, arriving from further east, made additional modifications. In A.D. 45 the Romans attacked Maiden Castle and last, but not least, a Romano-Celtic temple with a priest's house adjoining was built on the eastern summit. This relic of Neolithic Britain seems to have been finally abandoned during the 5th century A.D. after an interrupted occupation lasting over 2,500 years.[1]

Maiden Castle and similar hill fortresses belonged to the days before siege operations were conceivable, because the engine of war had not at that date arrived on the military stage in Britain. Therefore a determined onslaught with fierce hand-to-hand fighting was the only way of achieving a successful assault. The strength of such bastions depended on the intricacy of their defences; no attacking force, for instance, could have hoped to succeed in scaling the flanking banks and penetrating the walls of Maiden Castle. Singly, the attempt would have been suicide. There, both entrances were so cunningly concealed by overlapping ramparts that a hostile force bent on capture would, unless accompanied by an expert guide, almost certainly find itself in a cul-de-sac and be picked off one by one by the defenders on the ramparts. The steepness of the northern bank—some 60 feet high—constituted a formidable obstacle.

[1] The writer was on the plateau at Maiden Castle on March 4, 1940 when suddenly the air raid sirens wailed at Dorchester at 2.0 p.m. He could not help feeling that though the early Briton might have felt safe in his fortified enclosure his modern counterpart certainly would not, should a German plane zooming over the earthwork suddenly let loose a stream of bullets from its machine guns. In due course, the 'all-clear' sounded and on returning to Dorchester it was learned that it had merely been a practice test of the air-raid system.

Often in this type of stronghold the inner bank was re-inforced by a wooden stockade the posts of which were intertwined with a barrier of impenetrable thorns. The plateau behind the parapet of the bank, when there was more than one, was a valuable asset to the defenders affording them an advance post which gave them greater freedom of movement. The parapet or outer scarp of the outer ditch was often strengthened by a stockade of sharpened stakes. In this manner the impregnable character of the *enceinte* was assured; but further skill and ingenuity were lavished on the entrances of which there were usually more than one. At Maiden Castle, the path of entry was converted into a veritable labyrinth by multiplying the banks and ditches in a bewildering manner. Every inch of that circuitous route is guarded by tall ramparts. There were seven or eight points in its course at which a fatal error was possible and one, at least, where a band of attackers could rush headlong to destruction. The eastern entrance was equally well camouflaged and guarded by transverse banks so that both points of entry were hard to find. In other words, before the fortress itself could be scaled, the maze surrounding it had first to be successfully negotiated.

It was once thought that such prehistoric remains as Maiden Castle were merely refuges to which, in time of trouble, the plain dwellers betook themselves, their families and their flocks. Modern excavations and discoveries, however, show them to have been permanent centres of occupation where communities hoped to live free from marauders. Under the lawless conditions then prevailing, tribes made their habitation on high ground of natural strength capable of being further fortified by their own efforts.

The Romans brought new ideas of military architecture to Britain, including the introduction of dressed and cemented stone. Their whole concept of war was far more advanced than that of the Britons. They had developed siege operations to a marked degree of excellence and their military machines were powerful and efficient. Their walled strongholds were determined not only by rampart strength but also on the capacity of their soldiers to man them. Men, not fortresses, were the criteria of the Roman army; consequently their earthworks were far less imposing than those of the prehistoric Britons. Their camps and stations were usually surrounded by a fosse of no great depth, and the rare cases in which more than one ditch is indicated are those which face the exposed northern frontier of the country where the barbaric hordes might have been expected to attack and, if they did, could be checked by series of trenches either covered with brushwood or filled with sharpened stakes. Temporary camps, when necessary, were hastily constructed of earthwork banks, ditches and a parapet, but when camps were to be permanent a stone wall replaced the earthern bank. The greatest monument of the Roman occupation of Britain from the soldiering point of view is the great frontier wall stretching from the Tyne to the Solway Firth, though it was preceded by a turf *vallum* as a temporary measure till its masonry successor could be established. This is known as Hadrian's Wall.

This great erection is part of a complex of works reaching across the Tyne-Solway isthmus for a distance of 74¼ miles. It was built as a result of the Emperor Hadrian's visit to Britain in A.D. 122 when the decision to close the frontier against the wild tribes of the north was taken. The works include the wall with its milecastles or blockhouses and turrets, its forts, a *vallum* and a military road. As originally designed, the wall was to run from Newcastle to Bowness in Solway, east of the Irthing. It was to be of stone, ten feet broad and twenty feet high westward of the turf. Every mile a blockhouse of stone or turf was provided which served two stone turrets, one on either side. The wall was not intended as a defensive line but as a continuous pathway of patrol with a field of operations to the north, the patrols being strengthened by a fighting force along the Stanegate to the rear.

During its construction, however, three changes of plan were introduced: first, the decision to proceed with a narrower wall only 7½ feet broad; secondly, the addition of the *vallum*; and thirdly, the substitution of forts on the wall for those on the Stanegate. The *vallum* in its original state was a flat-bottomed ditch running without interruption behind the wall, 30 feet wide, with mounds on either side. It had no military value and its purpose appears to have been to seal off a military zone from the wall for the possible purpose of preventing deserters leaving the patrolling force. Each fort contained from 500 to 1,000 men. There were probably fifteen of these as originally planned. Communication was assured by a road on the south berm of the *vallum* with causeways at forts and blockhouses. At a later date, it was decided to extend the wall eastwards to Wallsend and replace the western wall of turf with one of stone, 9 feet thick, retaining the old turrets.

With the building of the Antonine Wall between the Firths of Forth and Clyde in A.D. 144 at the instigation of Antoninus Pius, Hadrian's Wall was abandoned. The Antonine Wall ran between Carriden and Old Kilpatrick, a distance of 37 miles and was guarded by nineteen forts. No doubt the shorter wall was considered advantageous as it required a smaller patrolling party and no blockhouse patrol. But Antonine's Wall, not proving the hoped-for success, was abandoned in turn in A.D. 200, and Hadrian's Wall came to life again after a lapse of 56 years and remained in being till it was finally given up in A.D. 383.

The Saxon invaders, who upset the even tenor of the Romano-British way of life, built little defensive stonework. They depended mainly on marsh and woodland for their protection. When, however, they did decide a line of continuous defence to be essential they built it of earth. Their great contributions to works of a defensive nature in Britain are four dykes; known as Offa's Dyke, Wansdyke, Bokerly Dyke and Wat's Dyke—the greatest of which is the first. Offa's Dyke, the largest lineal earthwork in this country, follows a line through the Welsh marches from the estuary of the Wye to that of the Dee. It was raised by Offa, King of Mercia in A.D. 779 to hold back the dispossessed Welsh from attacking the English settlers. This bastion is a plain bank and ditch and cannot in any way be regarded as a fortified line; rather is it a patrol highway after the style of Hadrian's Wall. Its length, about 120 miles, takes advantage of every natural feature to increase its usefulness. A large gap of 25 miles exists at its southern end where use is made of the river Wye from six miles above Hereford to near Monmouth; similarly, further on, 7 miles of the Severn are pressed into service.

All these fortified boundary lines pale into insignificance, however, when compared with the Great Wall of China completed in 211 B.C. This stupendous undertaking was carried out by Ch'in Shih Huiang Ti to keep out the barbarians from central Asia and consisted in linking the defensive walls built by Chinese frontier states and extending it eastwards till it reached the sea so as to form one continuous rampart of 1,500 miles. The height varies between 15 and 20 feet and the wall is crowned with towers and camps at intervals. It was built by conscript labour organized on a gigantic scale and its erection entailed terrible sufferings and many deaths. This construction did not prove a complete bar to invasion, but it acted as a serious obstacle to the horsemen of the steppes, prevented minor incursions and helped to stabilise the frontier. It was built of stone blocks, each measuring 14 inches by 7 inches by $3\frac{1}{2}$ inches and weighing 28 lb. One wonders whether there is any significance in the fact that all these figures are fractions or multiples of seven.

To switch for a moment to the modern world, the Maginot and Siegfried lines of World War II prove that this type of fortified wall to keep out invaders is not extinct.

Walled cities have been a feature of the landscape for thousands of years and reached their apex during the reign of military machines. The walled town, except as a showpiece of interest, gradually passed into oblivion as the power of artillery exerted itself and finally overcame even the strongest masonry.

CHAPTER VI

THE DEVELOPMENT OF THE STONE CASTLE

The castle was an important feature of the feudal system which, blossoming in France under the later Carolingian kings, reached England in the wake of William the Conqueror. Initially, the castle was the private property of a feudal lord designed primarily as a military stronghold and secondarily as a residence. Its introduction was the result of the consolidation of the feudal system. The territorial baron had four reasons for building it. It separated his dwelling from those of his vassals; it formed an impregnable strongpoint against his vassals' disaffection; it acted as a perpetual reminder to them of their dependence on him; and it withstood assaults from other lords who might wish to increase their standing at the expense of his own. The castle, therefore, either rose within, or in addition to, the *burgh* or settlement, or was erected, like the Peak castle in Derbyshire, on a lone site. In later cases, it often attracted a small community to seek shelter beneath its walls.

An unlimited number of castles presupposes an unlimited number of petty princelings who, taking the law into their own hands, were ever ready to try conclusions with one another. A multiplicity of castles, therefore, tended to lead to brigandage unless their owners could be controlled by their monarch; for the feudal lord was in theory the king's subject and his fortified stronghold belonged to his sovereign overlord. To combat this danger, Charles the Bald of France by his edict of Pistes in A.D. 864 took power to prohibit the raising of new castles without his sanction and to demolish those which had already been built without a royal licence. No such powers existed in England and another two and a half centuries were to elapse before the Crown assumed control. Except where anarchy already reigned, legislation of this character to safeguard the feudal system was enacted during the Middle Ages wherever that system formed the basis of the constitution. The king was the *de jure*, if not the *de facto*, owner of every castle in his realm. In parts of the continent, however, the absence of any national authority was responsible for the appearance of numerous castles, and the rivalry of neighbouring chieftains, together with the activities of robber barons, called for the construction of official fortresses to suppress them. Europe, from Portugal to Poland, is the graveyard of numberless castles, both great and small, which testify to the unsettled conditions of mediaeval times. In the Middle East, the Crusaders also erected immense structures, like the Krak des Chevaliers which was never subdued and the Kalat el Husn begun by Raymond IV, Count of Toulouse, in A.D. 1104. The Teutonic Order of Knights pursued the same policy in East Prussia.

The stone castle, developing directly from the fortified earthwork, consisted essentially of a strongpoint surrounded by curtain walls. Within this enclosure were one or two baileys in the inner of which were placed the living quarters of the castellan. Sometimes, these wards were surrounded by a moat and access was obtained through a gatehouse often defended by a drawbridge.

Although the castle became universal it reached its perfection in this country under the Norman, Angevin and Plantagenet kings who were the master builders of such fortifications. With few exceptions, their erection began under Henry II and culminated in the reign of Edward Longshanks. The latter's masterpieces were the high watermark of design, and the end of the 13th century ushered in the golden age of English military architecture.

Castles of the 11th and 12th centuries whether in Normandy or England were of two defined types: those with rectangular and those with shell keeps. The former were favoured when the site selected was new, the latter where a *motte* or mound already existed. Examples did occur where a rectangular keep was constructed on a previous encampment but the shell keep was never erected on a new location. This practice arose from the fact that the heavy rectangular keep could only be built with safety on solid ground, whereas an artificial mound was quite able to sustain the well-distributed weight of a shell keep. The latter were more numerous but being less robust than the former they have succumbed to the ravages of time and are now in a minority.

RECTANGULAR KEEP

The rectangular keep is the simpler in form, the grander in outline, the greater in passive strength and the more durable. It is usually the earlier in date and was normally built on the highest point in the bailey. Its dimensions vary; that of the White Tower in London is approximately 110 feet square and 90 feet high. The average thickness of its walls was between 7 and 18 feet. The exterior faces of a rectangular keep were usually relieved by slightly projecting pilasters. These flank each side and differ in number according to the size of the structure. All rose from a common plinth. Except in smaller keeps, the flanking pilasters protrude 8 or 10 feet above the parapet to form the outer faces of the roof turrets, the intermediate ones stopping just short of the base of the parapet. They are generally divided into stages to mark the internal floor levels. More diminutive keeps have only a basement and one floor, but in the larger structures a basement and three floors are common. The basement, about 12 to 15 feet in height and ventilated by narrow slits, is always at ground level and was invariably used as a storeroom.

Some keep walls are solid but most of them contain rooms intended as oratories, bedchambers and garderobes. The latter were provided with stone seats and the waste arrangements were generally vertical shafts in the wall or chutes leading to the outside face. Primitive fireplaces were installed on the principal floors with simple flues to assist smoke expulsion. A kitchen was usually in evidence though it hardly came up to modern standards. Cooking as an art had not developed by the 12th century and such meals as were required were probably prepared over a brazier. Some larger keeps included a chapel. The main floor in a big keep averaged 25 feet in length and was lit by two-foot windows often grouped under a single arch outside. The upper floor or floors were occasionally partitioned to give sleeping accommodation to the defenders.

Roofs were originally slanted at a moderate angle to allow rain to drain away into the gullies provided, but such a pitched construction prevented the installation of military machines. Later improvements dispensed with the gables and substituted a flat lead-covered platform which could permit the mounting of such engines. The floors of these keeps consisted of thick planks resting on joists of heavy timber which constituted a considerable fire risk. In most rectangular keeps there was an interior well-stair in one angle commencing at ground floor level which served every floor. This terminated on the roof under the turret head. In addition, there were other stone staircases which began at higher levels. A well was one of the most important adjuncts to a keep and at Dover there were two.

Great trouble was taken to protect the entrance, which was the weakest point in a keep's defences. A small rectangular tower was built on one side of the main structure about one third of the breadth and two thirds of the height of the actual keep. At one end at ground level commenced a straight stone stairway which rose to near the other end where it stopped at a landing which was the vestibule to the actual entrance. Above the lowest part of the stairway was a low tower and a strong doorway. Over the landing at the stairhead was a larger, stronger tower also guarded by a strong doorway. Outside the latter the stairway was broken by a drawbridge. The vestibule at the head of the stone steps was generally a good-sized vaulted chamber. In it was the main doorway into the keep. Sometimes, as at Dover, it contained a guardroom. The outer entrance consisted of one or two stout oaken doors reinforced by iron. These could be shut and barred by strong beams of oak. A portcullis was very seldom installed to deny entry into a keep.

Twelfth century keeps did not offer five-star accommodation. They were, in fact, extremely uncomfortable. It must be remembered, however, that such buildings were first and foremost fortresses and were meant for the lord and his armed retainers to live in only during a siege. It would seem that the owners who commissioned the designs of these keeps must have mistrusted their own followers almost as much as they feared their enemies. The staircases and galleries were often planned to restrict internal as well as external communication. The specially guarded entrance, the multiplicity of doors, the steep winding staircases and the sharp bends in the passages, though they might delay the entry of a foe and harass him if he gained admittance, also prevented the rapid ingress of the garrison. Movement was so hindered that if the outer bailey were taken by assault, the defenders had scarcely time to retreat into the keep which thus became liable to a *coup-de-main*. Given a sufficient and loyal garrison with an ample supply of stores and food, however, a Norman keep was well-nigh impregnable owing to its prodigious strength. The windows were too small and too high for their shutters to be endangered by fire-balls and the walls were too thick to be mined or breached. But from the defence point of view, a loop in a thick wall however well-splayed internally offered little scope for an archer's talents and the lower slits were only for air. A bow could be used with advantage from the larger windows higher up but the distance of the bowman from the ground detracted from his effectiveness. Rocks and stones flung from the roof by machines, where it had been adapted for such appliances, could have assisted the defence but they seem to have been rarely used. The defence measures adopted by the possessors of a rectangular keep, therefore, were based on passive principles which denied them the power of manoeuvre and crippled their initiative. It was the tactics of the hedgehog or the tortoise where the defenders awaited death from starvation or deliverance from without. It was a policy of inaction tinged with the philosophy of Micawber.

Such are the bare details of Norman rectangular keeps in England from the erection of the White Tower begun in A.D. 1078 to the building of Helmsley keep in Yorkshire in the year A.D. 1180.

SHELL KEEP

The plan and dimensions of a shell keep were governed by the topographical nature of the ground on which it was to be erected. Some were circular while others were polygonal in shape. Their diameter varied between 30 and 100 feet and their walls were generally about 8 to 10 feet thick. To prevent possible settlement, their walls were usually set back about 3 feet from the edge of the mound on which they were to stand. The interior of the larger examples was an open court in which buildings and sheds were placed against the ring wall. There were instances in which these open courts were roofed over. The approach to these keeps appears to have been by a wooden bridge over the surrounding ditch and thence by steps up the mound, though in some cases more elaborate precautions were taken including the addition of a drawbridge. It must be realised that these shell keeps and the mounds on which they stood formed part of the line of the castle's outer defences though isolated from them by their own ditch, often a part of the main moat of the stronghold. This type of keep also had its well. Besides other approaches, the curtain was always used as one way to the keep. It is a great pity that so few of these keeps have survived and those which have, have been renovated almost out of recognition, for as the representatives of an early form of fortification and as chief seats of ancient families, they possess an intrinsic charm. When extremely large, like those at Windsor and Arundel, such keeps have an air of stately beauty. Massive as the rectangular keep is and rugged in its grim features it lacks in some respects the grandeur and outline of the stern round tower of bygone days, identified as this was with the early residences of those hardy Norsemen who laid the foundations of the English speaking peoples.

The next development in castle construction is known as the Early English period, though the magic of the Norman keep remained so strong in England that it influenced castle builders throughout the reigns of Stephen and Henry II. The Early English style favoured more ornamentation and less severity in castle design. There were many castles built in this country during Stephen's reign referred to as *castra adulterina*. As they were destroyed by his successor, little is known about them. They obviously could not have been as robust as the earlier Norman keeps or their demolition would have proved more difficult; they were probably constructed of wood or were mere walled enclosures of little strength. Few, if any, represented the chief seats of large landowners, and being erected for the most part on new sites the earthworks surrounding them were inconspicuous; consequently, where the battlements above ground were levelled there was little left to indicate the spots where they once stood.

When both types of Norman keep fell into disfavour they were succeeded by cylindrical towers known as *donjons* or *juliets* and the style adopted corresponded to that of the middle period of Early English ecclessiastical architecture. This was scarcely an advance in military design as the defenders of an isolated round tower could not concentrate their fire and could only protect the foot of the wall by exposing themselves on the summit. As against that, given equally good material, the round tower was stronger, more difficult to breach and harder to destroy by mine. It was also capable of being vaulted in every story and, thus, was more rigid. Incidently, too, it was less liable to be damaged by fire.

These donjons or round towers were usually entered at first floor level, either by an exterior stone staircase or by a drawbridge which dropped into position on a detached pier whence a flight of steps descended to the ground. They normally contained three floors. The basement was as usual the storeroom; the central floor was the principal apartment, with a fireplace and sometimes mural chambers, one of which was a garderobe; and the upper floor was either a barrack-room or a bedroom for the lord. The walls were ordinarily about 10 to 12 feet thick and there was a well-stair. In the larger towers, such as at Coucy, built by Engerrand III, Sieur de Coucy, there was often a small chamber over the main entrance which housed the machinery for raising and lowering the portcullis. Occasionally, the main staircase began at ground level and ended on the first floor re-commencing on the opposite side for access to the top floor, a method of ascent borrowed from the earlier rectangular keep. This arrangement prevented anyone from leaving his post on the battlements without the knowledge of the lord who lived in the main chamber.

When the cylindrical tower acted as the donjon or 'keep' it was normally situated within the castle precincts, but there were exceptions both in France and England. At Coucy, for instance, the tower had its own ditch. Soon after round towers appeared they were adapted as mural towers flanking and strengthening the curtain wall. In this capacity they were employed especially to cap an angle or flank a doorway. Between 1170 and 1220, much was done to introduce more domestic comforts into castles. Fireplaces, which in Norman keeps were often mere lateral orifices for smoke vents, became better designed and constructed. The flues, too, were better able to cope with their task. In Norman keeps, wooden floors were essential, but with vaulted ceilings the floors of round towers could be compounded of beaten lime and sand. This excluded draughts and diminished the risk of fire. Halls, chapels and apartments also became more ornate as time progressed.

In addition to the flanking defence afforded by towers on the curtain wall, a contrivance called a *bretasche* was in general use. This was a covered timber gallery supported by struts resting on corbels running round the walls outside the battlements. In larger towers there were sometimes two tiers of these galleries, the upper projecting beyond the lower. This formed a formidable obstacle against attack. The *bretasche* was only erected on the approach of a siege, though at Chateau Gaillard built by Richard Coeur de Lion in France a similar arrangement was fashioned in stone. This formed machicolations through which the besieged could pour boiling oil and molten lead on the heads of the besiegers. It is not in England that the best examples of these Early English donjons are to be found. In France under Philip Augustus the new style of building was carried much further and the results were greatly superior; well-known instances being Coucy, Issoudun and Chateau Gaillard among others.

Henry III was a great patron of the arts, especially architecture, but his reign produced few notable castles with the exception of one which will be mentioned later. South Wales contains some fortresses which appear to have been built, though possibly on old sites, under Henry's authority. During his long reign both royal and baronial castles became more comfortable from the domestic standpoint. Large sums were spent on beautifying their interiors which added greatly to their desirability as residences. In fact, more attention began to be paid to luxury than to military necessity, for strongholds were allowed to fall into disrepair in times of peace and troops were often conspicuous by their absence.

Every castle containing more than one tower and having multiple lines of defence partook of a concentric nature though even in the largest of the earlier examples the secondary defences were of small extent and confined mainly to works for the protection of the entrance. It remained for the Edwardian castle to reach the apex in castle architecture. So great was the fame of Edward I that the concentric system, which he did not invent but adopted, has been bequeathed his name. Actually, Caerphilly, one of the finest specimens of the concentric castle in this island, was completed by a subject during the end of Henry's reign before Edward returned from the East. The term *Edwardian* has therefore been bestowed on that type of fortress which succeeded the round tower with its walled enclosure and brought the art of fortification from the Early English style to that of the decorated period of military architecture.

Edward's talents as a military engineer were mainly directed to North Wales. The fortifications in that principality in the last decades of the 13th century had been hill camps quite unfitted for the warfare of the time and out of keeping with the king's mode of operations. He found there neither English mounds nor Norman keeps and his works in that country were both original in conception and bold in execution. To him are due the castles of Conway, Caernarvon, Beaumaris and Harlech.

The first peculiarity of a concentric castle is the arrangement of its lines of defence, one within the other. With towers at the angles and along the walls, an Edwardian castle is so planned that no part is left entirely to its own resources. A wall cannot be adequately defended unless the exterior base of one portion can be seen and dominated from the summit of another. A Norman keep or Early English round tower could only be defended by men hurling missiles from the battlements, an activity which exposed them to as much danger as it did their assailants. The employment of mural towers, projecting as they did from the curtain wall, not only added to its strength but when placed within bowshot of one another, enabled the defenders, safely under cover, to enfilade the intermediate curtain and prevent a possible ram attack to which it was highly susceptible. At the same time, towers less perfectly flanked were, because of their shape and solidity, less liable to be breached. This ensured a saving of material, for the walls could be less thick. At the same time the defence as a whole could be carried out more skilfully and with less circumscription. In other words, it did allow the garrison to retain a certain amount of initiative and pass from a passive to an active form of defence. There was of course nothing new in this elementary principle of warfare but it had been forgotten or ignored in the designs of keeps, round towers, donjons and juliets.

The concentric system, however, accomplished more than this. The lines of defence were so arranged that the defenders could sally forth from one sector and harass the attackers in another. Moreover, each tower or gatehouse and sometimes even each whole part of a building was so contrived that it could be held as a separate operation for a short time. Also, from the arrangement of the lines, a breach in the outer wall did not necessarily involve the loss of the whole castle. In concentric castles the keep—the main feature in earlier types of fortresses—was replaced by an open courtyard or inner ward strengthened at its sides by gatehouses and mural towers. Along the sides of this enclosure were built the hall, chapel and other domestic quarters. Around this walled inner ward was a narrow second ward which was broken up into compartments by cross walls containing gates rather like the watertight doors and compartments in a modern ship. This arrangement isolated any body of attackers who might have breached the outer walls. The narrowness of this second ward exposed any assailants who might have gained entrance to an assault from either flank and prevented them from obtaining reinforcements or setting up engines of war. Beyond the second ward was usually a third or outer ward, an area of considerable size which enabled a large part of the garrison, the horses and, in cases of emergency, the neighbouring peasants with their flocks and herds to be lodged. The outer ward often contained a moat or large sheet of water formed by damming back some local rivulet. In such cases, the defence of the dam was of prime importance and was specially catered for by stout walls along its length with towers or gatehouses at either end. In concentric castles all parts were intended for everyday use. No portion was allotted for siege purposes only. The hall, chapel and kitchen were in constant use and were constructed on a scale worthy of the occasion.

. An Edwardian gatehouse was an imposing structure, usually rectangular in plan, flanked in front by two drum towers and sometimes supported in rear by two others containing well staircases. In its centre was the portal arch opening into a long straight passage which traversed the building. Three loops in each flanking tower commanded the bridge of approach, raked the lateral curtain and covered a point immediately outside the gate. Above the portal was a small window and at the summit a machicolation set out on corbels. Alternatively, a kind of bridge was sometimes thrown from drum tower to drum tower a couple of feet in advance of the stonework leaving a gap through which stones and even beams could be dropped on the heads of those who might be assailing the gate below. The portal arch, wide enough to admit a waggon or three men abreast, was usually of the form known as 'drop'. Within the first defence was a portcullis and behind it a two-leaved door opening outwards capable of being fastened by one or two stout oaken baulks which could be pushed into cavities in the wall when not in use. Behind this door the vaulting was replaced by a flat timber ceiling through which a second portcullis could descend. Then came two lateral doorways opening into the porter's lodge and a small room. Generally, in addition to these gates and doors the vault was pierced with several holes about twelve inches across called *meurtrières*. These served either to hold posts to check the ingress of possible attackers, or to enable pikes to be thrust down upon their heads. The first floor of the larger gatehouses contained a handsome chamber with lateral doors leading to the ramparts of the curtain and, occasionally to an oratory as well. The portcullises were worked from this apartment.

The walls of Edwardian castles varied between 25 and 40 feet in height and were from 6 to 8 feet thick. On their top was a path called the *allure* or rampart walk protected in front by an embattled parapet and in rear by lower and lighter walls. The ramparts were normally reached from adjacent mural towers but in some cases by an open stairway of stone. Mural towers differed a good deal in size and form but were usually round or half-round. Where there was an outer ward and a second wall this was considerably lower than the inner curtain which commanded it, and the mural towers in the outer wall were of the same height as that of the wall itself. The barbican was sometimes a mere walled space in front of the gateway at the end of the bridge.

The castles of Henry III and Edward I combined the palace and the fortress, but although domestic arrangements had become almost lavish according to the standards of the day they were always subordinated to military needs. Considering their date, sanitary methods were quite good, the number of garderobes and disposition of waste material being adequate for 13th century hygiene.

The Edwardian castle, a magnificent architectural achievement, was the swan-song of castle building. Later ones were erected but they were pygmies compared with their predecessors. For another hundred years these proud examples of military engineering kept their enemies at bay and defied man's efforts to destroy them. Then the gun, feeble though it was, appeared before them. The tocsin sounded the changed circumstances. Castles became increasingly vulnerable as the power of artillery grew and those which had stood erect and undismayed when the cannon's roar first shattered the silence of the hills, battled on bloody but unbowed till at last they crumbled into dust under the weight of bombardment. Like the engines of war which attacked them and the cross-bowmen who defended them, they had because of their massive strength lingered on into an age alien to their purpose. Those which remain to gladden our eyes have been repaired and maintained for special purposes and they stand today as mute witnesses of the days of feudalism in a world which has passed them by.

CHAPTER VII

THE CHARIOT, HORSE FURNITURE AND CAVALRY

Man employs the horse in three capacities: as a pack animal, a draught animal and a mount; but only the last two were normally connected with war till the appearance of the internal combustion engine at the beginning of the 20th century practically drove the horse from the field. The second method of employment may be divided into two categories, combat and movement of material; the latter covering ammunition, supply and baggage trains sometimes referred to as the second and third lines of transport. The only means of utilising a draught horse in battle was to harness it to a chariot, a form of cart which for all practical purposes disappeared some 2,000 years ago. The chariot itself had two applications: as a fighting vehicle and as a triumphal car; or, to put it into 17th century English, 'as well for Warr as Tryumph'.[1] We are concerned only with its first aspect.

The war chariot was a primitive form of fighting carriage. It could almost be said to have been the armoured car of the ancient world. It was used in the Egyptian, Assyrian, Greek, Persian and other armies. The original Assyrian chariot, heavy and cumbersome lacked mobility and it was eventually replaced by a lighter model with beneficial results but most forms, following the usual design, were swift and manoeuvrable. The ordinary wooden chariot consisted of a movable platform about sixteen inches above the ground having two wheels of four spokes each mounted on an axle under the platform. It was open at the back but protected at the front and sides by a continuous shield built into the bodywork. It was normally drawn by two horses, one on each side of the pole, though a third and even a fourth animal could be attached by traces should additional speed be required. The usual detachment

---

[1] In the warrant dated 11th August 1688 appointing Sir Martin Beckman Controller of Fireworks in Tower Place, Woolwich, he is styled 'Comptroller of ffireworks as well for Warr as Tryumph'.

was two men, an archer and a driver, though a third was sometimes carried as a protection for the bowman when firing. The commander of the vehicle was always the archer, who was responsible for issuing orders to the charioteer. Both Persians and Britons had blades or scythes fixed to the ends of the axle-tree for the purpose of cutting down their adversaries as they drove through the opposing enemy.

Early man rode bareback, using an elementary form of bridle. This is corroborated by the fact that Assyrian bas-reliefs represent neither a saddle not a stirrup and that Egyptian monuments only depict the horse when harnessed to a chariot. The Greeks possessed few cavalry and no word in their language to convey the meaning of riding, so it must be presumed that the early races of Europe had no knowledge of the saddle till the Romans wrote about it in the 4th century B.C. As a stirrup without a saddle is like Hamlet without a Prince of Denmark, it can be assumed that both were comparatively late arrivals among articles of horse furniture. The spur, therefore, took pride of place after the bridle.

The origin of the bridle is hidden in the slipstream of time and it is impossible even to suggest a date for its appearance. It must in the first instance have formed part of the thongs of sinew which did duty as reins. The bridle proper, a word derived from the Celtic *brid*, consists of a head-stall with a frontal, the bit and reins. The bit may be solid or made in two parts linked together, and could not have come into existence till the advent of the Bronze Age. The snaffle appeared later. The Roman bit was a thin solid bar of iron with a ring attached at each end to accommodate the reins. In due course the jointed bit was developed and some of these had branches; in other words the snaffle emerged. Although bridles differed in detail in various parts of the world, the general design was basically the same.

Man having learned to subjugate the horse, it would have occurred to him that some sort of goad attached to his foot would offer advantages, not only in controlling his mount but in freeing his hands for other tasks particularly in war. Having conceived the idea, the best way of implementing it was to devise some sort of contrivance consisting of arms and leathern thongs to embrace his heel with a sharp point projecting backwards to prick the horse's flank. This instrument has remained unaltered, save in detail, to the present day.

The evolution of the spur was a gradual process and changes in design were slow. Some took place owing to alterations in armour, some to modifications in saddles and some even to mere caprices of fashion. They varied from the short spike of Roman times through the elaborations of the 15th and 16th centuries to the restrained patterns of our own day. The most startling innovation was the substitution of the revolving rowel for the simple spike, a process which took almost a hundred years to complete. Originally, spurs were regarded as a useful means of assisting a rider and when not in use were put away for a future occasion; but it was reserved for the Middle Ages to invest the spur with an emblematic significance far beyond its natural purpose. This romantic outlook was largely responsible for the flamboyant designs produced during that period. Some consider this suggestion overrated and in support of their contention point to the fact that Chaucer in his *Canterbury Tales* makes only one reference to the spur and that not relating to a knight. In describing *The Good Wyf*, written about A.D. 1370 he says 'and on her feet a paire of spores sharpe'. On the other hand, accounts do go to prove that spurs were intimately linked with knighthood. We talk of one 'winning his spurs', and the ceremonies connected with the donning of spurs at a knight's investiture and the severance of them on the occasion of his degradation do highlight the fact that spurs once had a value far beyond that of mere utility.

In *How Knyghtis of ye Bathe shulde be mayd* written in the early part of the 15th century 'the Squyers' are directed 'to their [The Knights'] swerdis, and a payre of gilt sporis, hangynge upon the hyltis of the same sworde, and shall bear the sworde with the sporis before them'. Also, in *The Booke of Honor and Armes*, printed in A.D. 1590 there is a chapter explaining 'The manner of makying knyghts about the yere of Our Lord, 1020'. After the details of administering certain oaths it says 'There came unto the Knyght seuen noble maidens, attyred in white, and girt his sword unto his side. That being done, foure knights of the most honourable in that presence, put on his spurres.' Regarding degradation, the same book states 'In the raigne of King Edward IV, it appeared a knight was degraded in this sort. First, after the publication of his offence, his gilt spurres were beaten from his heels, then his sword was taken from him and broken. That being done, eurie peece of his armour was brused, beaten and caste aside.' After which he was hanged. In several other old documents there are allusions to a knight's spurs on his degradation being hacked off by the king's master cook with his cleaver.

Spurs are not mentioned in the Bible nor have the Egyptians left any record of them in their tombs nor on their monuments. Homer, though he gives detailed descriptions of arms and armour in the *Iliad*, omits any reference to the spur. It is true that Xenophon and other writers of his time allude to something which could have been a spur when they used a word meaning a gadfly but it is questionable whether the spur in the accepted sense of the word is intended. Theophrastus,[1] however, places the matter beyond doubt in his *Character Studies* when he describes a vain petty little man as one who would walk about in his spurs. Strangely enough, *Punch* thousands of years later expressed the same sentiments when it depicted such a person as 'the footiest man on an 'orse and the 'orsiest man on foot'. Cicero, Livy and other Latin writers mention spurs, but no representation of them exists on Roman sculptures.

In all probability, the earliest form of spur was made of two pieces of hard wood or bone, or a combination of both, sharpened at one end and bound to the foot by lengths of sinew. A similar type is found today among some native tribes in Patagonia who spend much of their time hunting a large swiftly running bird from the saddle. A somewhat analogous wooden spur is portrayed on a Greek vase of about the 5th century B.C. The Patagonian spur consists of two pieces of hard wood, six inches long, connected about the middle by a short piece of leather about two inches in length. This leather is adjusted to the heel and the two bits of wood being placed one on each side of the foot, the front ends are drawn towards each other by a leathern thong passed over the instep, under the sole and bound round the foot. This keeps the

---

[1] A Greek philosopher, a native of Eresos in the island of Lesbos. Born 382 B.C. He was, in addition, an author, a botanist, a mineralogist, a musician, a meteorologist and a natural history expert.

two pieces of wood in position with their hinder ends approaching one another behind the heel. A sharp iron point is inserted in each of the ends.

The earliest bronze spurs appear to date from the 3rd century B.C. They all presented the same characteristics—a short plain point about half an inch in length with short side-pieces projecting forward about two inches on each side of the foot. The sides were circular in section though often flattened slightly on the inside with a spread just sufficient to embrace a bare heel. The button-shaped studs at the ends of the side-pieces designed for the attachment of straps were similar to those of a modern spur. Strangely enough, this stud disappeared before the beginning of the Christian era and did not re-appear till the middle of the 18th century. Why this simple and efficacious method of attaching the strap to the spur remained in abeyance for over 1,700 years is a mystery. It suited its purpose admirably, so why abandon it?

About the 5th century A.D. when iron had replaced bronze the spike of the spur became longer often achieving a length of five inches. This type of spur lacked any guard against undue penetration of the horse's side should the rider's foot be forced against his mount in the heat of battle. This undoubtedly did happen as the next change was to make the neck of the spur two inches long and blunt, and to insert into it a short spike thus allowing the flattened end of the neck to act as a safeguard against excess entry. Another pattern with the same end in view was the ball and spike type in which the ball acted as a guard. In due course steel superseded iron in spur production.

The rowel spur probably came over from the continent and may have been introduced into this country from France by Simon de Montfort who arrived in England in A.D. 1238. He claimed the earldom of Leicester *jure matris* and married Eleanor, sister of Henry III. It is thought that he may have induced the king to make the change because Henry's first seal shows the prick spur whereas his second seal features the rowel spur. After its introduction, the rowel spur changed in appearance during the next couple of centuries. Sometimes, the rowels were small and the necks long, at others the rowels were large and the necks short. Fashion probably was responsible for these modifications. As the centuries passed the tendency to decorate spurs became more and more marked. This ornamentation was introduced to keep pace with a similar trend in armour. It was a form of exhibitionism which became very prevalent during the heyday of armour, and one might say that during the ornate period of the latter the simple purpose of the spur became overlooked. In this connection it is interesting to note that, in the Royal Artillery, spurs for the field officer's mess-kit were once gilt. When plate armour claimed the limelight the spur was often riveted to the steel covering of the foot and the strap became superfluous. When armour in due course was dethroned by the firearm and men's apparel became less fancy, the spur slid back into its old contour. Basically, therefore, with the exception of the rowel, there is little difference between the spur today and that of the Roman horseman.

The saddle was certainly known among the nomads of Asia in the 4th century before Christ as the Chertomlyk vase testifies, but the first description of it comes from the pen of Zonaras, a Byzantine historian of the 12th century in his account of the struggle in A.D. 340 between Constans and Constantine, sons of Constantine the Great. The latter on his death left his vast empire in equal portions to his three sons. The afore-mentioned brothers fought over their inheritance with dire results for Constantine who met his death in this fratricidal affair. The use of the saddle in Scandinavia dates back to the 5th century A.D. The war saddle has altered remarkably little during the last 2,000 years except that the cantle has been lowered. The German saddle of the 9th century is almost indistinguishable from that of the nomad of central Asia but the Norman was more pretentious in appearance. During the 13th and 14th centuries the saddle in Europe did assume a more chair-like form but it was a passing phase. Subsequently, the saddle regained its more sober outline.

The stirrup is said to have originated in Assyria about 850 B.C. and was doubtless adopted by the peoples of central Asia who passed most of the day in the saddle. It was introduced into Europe by the Huns. It conferred a great advantage on the cavalryman who, with its assistance, could wield his lance or sword with one hand, hold his shield and reins with the other and at the same time remain firmly seated in the saddle. The stirrup was one of the main reasons why the Goths were able to rout the Roman army at Adrianople in A.D. 378. The shape of the stirrup has varied during the course of its history. Initially, it was a looped leathern strap from the saddle into which the rider could slip his foot, and to which was subsequently added a wooden or metal plate. The stirrup afterwards assumed a circular or triangular form. Since its object was to support the rider's foot the latter configuration was the better pattern. Not content with this, the horseman of later times used a type resembling a metal box with triangular sides. The various shapes seem to have been the result of individual fancy rather than of any conscious development in design. In later years the stirrup became less ornate and tended to adopt the form it assumes today. There were two types of stirrup which had additional features. One, the *pyrophore*, had a lantern in it to serve the purpose of lighting the rider's path and warming his feet. The other was a stirrup with a rowel on its inner side thus obviating the wearing of a spur. This is found in Greece and is thought to be of eastern origin and so may possibly be an interesting remnant of Persian influence left behind after the wars of long ago.

Cavalry played a large part in warfare during the early Middle Ages. They were instrumental in altering the strategy of campaigning and the tactics of the battlefield. The mounted hordes which debouched on to central and southern Europe in the 4th and 5th centuries A.D. when the Roman Empire was in decline created havoc and death among the people. Northern Europe fathered the Vandals and the Goths and the plains of central Asia bred the Huns and the Mongols. Between them they changed the character of mediaeval Europe and established cavalry as a dynamic force in war. Horsemen are the offspring of the empty waste lands where the wild horse roams at will; they are not the children of the crowded cities nor of the bazaars of the East. Conditions must be right for a band of embryonic cavalry to develop and these in olden times were mainly to be found in northern Europe and the plains of central Asia. Horsemanship is radically a nomadic characteristic and horsemastership a wanderer's tradition; so to trace the birth and development of cavalry at its source the nomads' way of life must be studied.

True nomads are found mainly in central Asia where they arrived about 800 B.C. and settled in the rolling plains; others like the *bedouin* are to be seen in Arabia and along the shores of north Africa. The former needed vast spaces for their settlements as they lived by pasturing cattle. True nomads must not be confused with wandering tribes such as the gipsies or aborigines of Australia who, because of some particular skill, adopt an itinerant life to enable them to trade. The essence of nomadism is migration for purposes of animal husbandry. Although the nomad found little restriction in his movements in pursuit of his way of life he was subject to certain limitations. Boundaries between the several tribes were clearly defined and jealously defended. During spring and early summer, of course, when pasture was abundant over wide areas, the only requisite was a readiness to move at short notice; but during winter when fodder and water were at a premium claims to share these sparse commodities were fiercely contested. It was these circumstances which made nomadism such a highly specialised scheme of existence. It was an end in itself not a mere wanderlust in search of food and cultivation.

The nomad, in fact, was no cultivator, he neither tilled nor sowed; he was *par excellence* the stockbreeder of the ancient and mediaeval worlds. His knowledge of domestication acquired through hunting and capture enabled him to build up immense herds of reindeer, cattle, sheep, goats, camels, yaks and horses. His style of living was dependent on the condition of these animals especially the latter which were the very core of his existence. Nomads, therefore, had to be always ready to pack up their belongings, round up their beasts and collect their families in order to seek fresh pastures. A good transport system combined with a strict code of discipline was essential if such an operation were to proceed smoothly. For life to be tolerable under such conditions, the tribe had to be organised on a military footing and be ready for attack or defence as occasion arose. To move camp periodically entailed a large number of horses and carts, so the nomad primarily employed the horse as a draught animal and not as a mount. The organisation of a nomad community, therefore, resembled that of an army; easily marshalled, self-supporting and capable of fighting under its elected leader. Riding was a secondary accomplishment but one well-suited to the conditions of life. Boys trained since childhood in the saddle had, under their strict precepts, the makings of a superb cavalry force. It is no wonder, therefore, that such bands in time formed some of the greatest cavalry races of the world and that in future years Europe was to experience periodic invasions of mounted warriors emanating from the Asiatic continent.

To close this chapter some words of Ammianus Marcellinus are appropriate. Describing the Huns he says:

'They are small, squat and beardless with horrible faces. They might be called beasts on two feet rather than human beings. Their apparel consists of a linen coat, the fur of wild rats and goat-skins round their legs. Riveted to their horses, there they eat, there they drink, there they sleep bent on the lean necks of their mounts, there they hold counsel. They neither cook nor season their food, and none of them ever touches a plough. They have no houses and are for ever on the move. Their wives and children follow them in carts.'

What better picture of the natural cavalryman could be found?

CHAPTER VIII

KNIGHTHOOD

Knighthood, the roots of which lie buried in the distant past, is a venerable and widespread institution. Horsemanship in the ancient world was considered to be not only a noble art but the prerogative of birth and wealth. Greek poets were fain to describe their heroes as skilled horsemen and the term *ruler of the steed* was frequently used to denote high rank and martial prowess. Notwithstanding this, however, the Greeks were woefully deficient in cavalry and usually hired their mounted troops from Thessaly. This lack of national horsemen undoubtedly explains why such a highly esteemed office never carried a title of honour as it did in Rome.

Legend says that an equestrian order in Rome can be traced to Romulus who selected a hundred distinguished and accomplished young men from each of the three tribes into which he had divided his people to act as a personal mounted bodyguard. Be that as it may, an order of knighthood appears to have existed by the reign of Servius Tullius who placed the official state horsemen on a statutory basis, increased their number, apportioned a certain sum for each 'knight' to purchase his horse and levied a tax for their maintenance. A certain amount of property was essential to qualify an aspirant for this rank and the sum varied from time to time. During the Empire it was fixed at 400 sesterces. At that period in Roman affairs, however, when probity and morals were at a discount, anyone who could qualify financially could be received into the order regardless of his worth; but in the days of the republic when integrity was still counted among the virtues none whose conduct might bring disgrace upon the whole body was allowed to continue as a member and none could be admitted whose nature did not measure up to the high standards required.

The privileges of a Roman knight were the presentation of a horse provided by public funds, the wearing of a gold ring placed on his finger at his adoption, a special tunic adorned with purple and a separate enclosure at the public games. An annual parade for Roman knights was held on the 15th July. They proceeded from the Temple of Mars outside Rome to the Capitol, mounted on their chargers, clad in their scarlet togas, crowned with olive wreaths and carrying their military insignia. Every fifth year this procession was of particular importance for, instead of being a mere spectacle for the Roman citizen, it assumed the character of a judicial investigation in which the censor received a report on the knights' conduct. Each knight stood at the rostrum while his fate was being decided. Those who had allowed their financial status to drop below the prescribed limit, who had neglected their horses or had behaved in a scandalous manner were ordered to sell their mounts. This was tantamount to degradation. Those, on the other hand, who had upheld the traditions of the order were confirmed in their rank for a further five years. This order of Roman knighthood, though similar in many respects to those of future centuries, was not their progenitor. It became extinct before mediaeval European orders arose.

The manner of conferring knighthood has varied in divers countries at different times, but it became more of an ordination than a simple act when the Church became closely connected with it, especially on the continent. Then, instead of the brief form of earlier centuries when the sovereign created a knight by putting a military belt over his shoulder, kissing his left cheek and saying 'In honour of the Father and the Son and of the Holy Ghost, I make you a knight', the preparations occupied a considerable time. Intending knights had to prepare themselves by abstinence and clean living. Fasts and vigils preceded the day of admission and the aspirant took a bath as a sign of purification and was arrayed in a white garment to signify the new life he had chosen. When the day of installation arrived the candidate was conducted in pomp to the cathedral or church where he was to be invested. The words used at this ceremony bore a strong resemlance to those spoken in the order of baptism. Afterwards, he was given his sword and spurs, and his cheek or shoulder was lightly touched to betoken the last insult he was to endure. Then he offered on the altar his sword which, after being blessed by the priest, was restored to him. Finally, he took an oath to speak the truth, maintain the right, succour the distressed, protect the innocent, practise courtesy, oppose the infidel, despise the allurements of the flesh and in all circumstances vindicate his honour.

Such were the ceremonies which in the days of holy wars attended the creation of a knight; but as conditions changed, religious intolerance grew less violent and the military qualifications connected with early knighthood became less important, the solemnity of the occasion reverted into a simple act in which the monarch touched the shoulder of the kneeling knight-designate with a sword and said *Sois chevalier au nom de Dieu*, 'I dub thee knight' or 'Arise, Sir Knight'. He who conferred the honour of knighthood became in a sense the father of him whom he had just honoured. Thus the grantee was considered to be adopted by the grantor. The Latin word *adoptatus* entering our language through the word *adobato* has been corrupted into 'dub', a term still in use in 'dubbing a knight'.

On the reverse side of the coin, a knight who had misbehaved himself or otherwise forfeited the respect which was his due, could be degraded in a highly unpleasant manner.

Fig. 46.—A Merovingian knight of the 8th century.

The military organisation of the Carolingian Empire and of the Saxon Heptarchy in England had proved incapable of stemming the invading hordes, mostly light horsemen, who swarmed over Europe during the first four or five centuries of the Christian era. It therefore became obvious that if defence in the future was to be effective it must be based on local considerations and that the essential military deterrent had to be the armoured cavalryman; in other words, the knight. The knight was specially trained and dedicated to the art of war and thus became an important military figure when light first began to filter into the Dark Ages. By the year A.D. 1000 this had resulted in much of Europe being parcelled out into small estates, each providing sufficient rent for a knight to support his family, devote his time to his profession and, if need arose, proceed to war under the banner of the overlord whose tenant he was. In this manner, a knightly class of highly efficient armoured cavalry was built up in Europe.

Knight service was introduced into England by William the Conqueror, at which time it was said that the kingdom contained 60,211 knights' fees. The value of land which constituted a knight's fee varied at different times. In the reign of Henry III, £15 p.a. was the accepted figure. By the reign of Edward II this sum had increased to £20 p.a. and by the reign of Edward IV to £40 p.a. Inflation is not a peculiarity of the 20th century.

Knights in England were formerly divided into two classes: *knights banneret* and *knights bachelor*. The name *banneret* is most probably derived from 'banner', a square flag. It has been affirmed that the privilege of the square flag belonged properly to a baron and therefore the knight banneret must have occupied an intermediate rank between a baron and a simple knight and have had some baronial privileges. The title did not occur in this country till the time of Edward I. The title of knight banneret was always a military honour bestowed on the field of battle. The recipient presented his flag to the commander who cut off its skirt and returned it as a square to its owner, in which form it became the emblem of his new dignity. The title gave the right to bear supporters and, as a distinguishing badge, his arms were emblazoned on a banner placed between the paws of his supporters. In England, the title of knight banneret was for life only; in France it was hereditary. When the order of baronets was instituted by James I, the title of knight banneret became redundant and the last person on whom it was conferred in the traditional manner was Sir John Smith who recovered the royal standard after the battle of Edge-

1. Scandinavian warrior; end of the eleventh or beginning of the twelfth century, from a sculpture in wood on the door of a church in Iceland, preserved in the Museum of Copenhagen. The equipment is remarkable by the conical casque with nose-piece and neck-covering, and by the curved sword or *glaive* which the warrior bears along with the buckler on his right shoulder.
2. Count of Barcelona, Don Ramon Berenger IV. (1140); from an engraved seal. The conical helmet has a nose-piece, and the rest of the armour seems to consist of a hauberk with hood, and breeches and leggings of mail, all in one piece. The long shield has a coat of arms on one of his seals, and stripes cn the other. The lance has a pennant.

Fig. 47.—A Scandinavian warrior of the 11th century.

hill in 1642. George III made a half-hearted attempt to revive it in 1773 when at a naval review at Portsmouth he conferred under the royal standard the title of knight banneret on Admirals Pye and Spry and on Captains Knight, Bickerton and Vernon.

Knight bachelor was a lower rank of knighthood than knight banneret, and the word 'bachelor' is said to be a corruption of the term *bas chevalier*. It had no bearing on the knight's matrimonial

Fig. 48.—An English knight armed with a martel; 13th century.

status. When the knight banneret fell into abeyance, the word 'bachelor' dropped out of use; since when the simple appellation of 'knight' has been used. Those in England entitled to the prefix 'Sir' are either baronets, simple knights or knights of one of the English orders of Chivalry.

The oldest order of Chivalry in the world is that of the Order of the Garter founded by Edward III in 1348. Since this date is outside the time scale of this book, it can be said that no such orders were in existence when the gun first made its appearance. There have been, however, over the course of years hundreds of orders of knighthood in Europe; many are defunct but a considerable number still flourish. To list them would be tedious and to describe each of them in turn would place an intolerable strain on the patience of the reader. There are, however, three which for historic reasons do merit attention. One has been suppressed, one is extinct and the other still maintains a precarious existence. These are: The Knights Templars; The Teutonic Order of Knights; and The Knights Hospitallers of St. John of Jerusalem.

THE KNIGHTS TEMPLARS

The Knights Templars were founded in 1119 by Hugh de Peganes and Godfrey de St. Amor who with seven others went to the Holy Land and formed themselves into a brotherhood for protecting pilgrims proceeding to the Holy Sepulchre, taking up arms against the infidels in concert with the Knights Hospitallers and guarding the Temple of Solomon. Baldwin II, King of Jerusalem, looked favourably on them and assigned them lodgings in his palace adjoining the Temple. Hence their name. The order was confirmed by Pope Honorius II in 1128. Notwithstanding the assistance they received from Baldwin and the Patriarch Guarimond, they were obliged to accept alms during their first nine years. They wore linen coifs and red caps, shirts of mail and a sword girded about them with a broad belt. Over all they had a white cloak reaching to the ground carrying on the left shoulder a red cross conferred on them by Pope Eugenius. Unlike the members of most military orders who were shaved, the Templars wore long beards.

In time, they became famous for their exploits against the Saracens on land and sea and thus won the hearts of Christian princes who showered vast revenues on them. They therefore became numerous and very wealthy. They transferred their allegiance to the Pope and withdrew their obedience from the

Patriarch of Jerusalem. Under their new overlord, however, they were accused of infamous crimes and their wealth exciting the cupidity of the French kings numbers were tried, condemned and burned alive or hanged in 1308–10 and the order suffered much persecution throughout Europe. Sixty-eight knights were burned at Paris in 1310. The order was finally condemned in 1312 by the Council of Vienne, part of its revenues being allocated to other orders, and abolished by Pope Clement V in April 1312. Jacques de Molay, the last grand master, was burned at the stake in Paris on 18th March 1314.

The Templars were spread over several countries and arrived in England some time prior to 1185. Their first London settlement was at Holborn, but their chief residence in the reign of Henry II was the Temple in Fleet Street, which they erected. They also built a church designed after the style of the Temple at Jerusalem and had it dedicated to God and Our Blessed Lady by Heraclius, Patriarch of Jerusalem, in 1185. By command of Edward II and by order of a papal bull, the English Knights Templars were cast into prison in 1307, and under a general council held in London their possessions were seized and handed over to the Crown. The head of the order in England died in the Tower of London. On the suppression of the order all their remaining assets were handed over to the Knights Hospitallers.

THE TEUTONIC ORDER OF KNIGHTS

The Teutonic Order of Knights is said to have owed its existence to the piety of a German and his wife who during the Crusades lived in Jerusalem and founded a hospital for the sick. Joined by others, this charitable organisation grew and in 1191 was constituted under the name of the Teutonic Order of Knights. The order was confirmed by Pope Celestin III who in a papal bull gave them permission to elect a master from among their members. Whereupon, Henry de Wallpot was elected grand master. About 1230, Conrad, Duke of Swabia, invited the Teutonic brethren to Prussia and assigned them the territory of Culm. Soon afterwards, ceasing to have any regard for their charitable origin, they grew extremely powerful and seized Prussia, building the towns of Elburg, Marienburg, Thorn, Danzig and Koenigsberg. Afterwards they subdued Livonia.

These knights wore a white mantle and had assigned to them for a badge by the Emperor Henry VI a cross potent, sable, to which John, King of Jerusalem, added a cross double potent, gold. The Emperor Frederic bestowed on them an imperial eagle and St. Louis of France augmented their badge with a chief, azure, semée of fleurs-de-lis.

This very powerful military order, however, did not retain its vast possessions for long. Its territories were invaded and its army defeated with great slaughter near Tannenberg by Jagellon, Duke of Lithuania, on 15th July 1410, and the grand master and many of the knights were slain. A large part of their property was incorporated into Poland in 1466 and into Brandenburg about 1521. Subsequently the order became divided into two branches, one situated at Morgenheim in Germany and the other at Utrecht. In 1525, the grand master was made a prince of the empire and the order became further weakened. By the Treaty of Pressburg dated 26th December 1805, the grand mastership was attached to the Imperial House of Austria. In 1809, its remaining possessions were appropriated by Napoleon. Thus passed into oblivion one of the most powerful military orders in history. Although its body died its spirit lingered on. From 1527 when the Emperor Charles V confirmed the grand mastership of the order with a seat beyond Prussia, the highest representatives of the order adopted the title *Hoch Und Deutschmeister*. This title was accepted by the House of Hapsburg, their members continuing to bear this honour down to 1923. Even after this date the order did not finally disappear, but was modified in 1929 into an organisation having religious tendencies. After World War II, its activities were revived in Austria, Italy and Germany.

THE KNIGHTS HOSPITALLERS

The Knights Hospitallers of St. John of Jerusalem led a peripatetic existence and a shadow of the former order still survives in Rome. Some merchants of Malfi, obtaining leave from the Caliph of Egypt to build a house in Jerusalem upon payment of tribute for themselves and their compatriots who might wish to go on a pilgrimage, erected two oratories and received pilgrims in accordance with their purpose. This charitable type of work appeared capable of expansion and it was extended to include attendance on the sick. A hospital was therefore founded and at the same time a church dedicated to St. John was built. The community therefore in 1099 took the title of Hospitallers of St. John of Jerusalem. After the Crusaders had conquered the Holy Land these 'male nurses' undertook further duties such as actively assisting pilgrims by binding themselves under oath to protect them in every way against the Saracens. This alteration, which took place in 1104, converted them into a semi-military order. They therefore added 'Knights' as a prefix to their title.

Their first head, Gerhard, who did not assume the title of grand master, ruled the fraternity from 1099 to 1118, and in the latter year Raymond Dupuy became the first grand master and, with the consent of Pope Bonifice, gave the Order its first written statutes. When the infidel finally overran the Holy Land the Hospitallers had to vacate Jerusalem and retire to Acre in 1290. After a few months they moved on to Cyprus having been welcomed there by John, King of Cyprus, who gave them Limassol. Here they remained for twenty years. In 1310, under the grand mastership of Foulques de Villeret they conquered Rhodes, settled down in their new home and became known as The Knights of Rhodes.

The Turks, however, captured Rhodes in 1522 and the knights had to beat a hasty retreat to Candia and Sicily where Pope Adrian VI granted them the city of Viterbo. They remained there till 1530 when the Emperor Charles V having conquered Malta offered it to the knights as a permanent home. The offer was gratefully accepted and in Malta the knights, who thereupon changed their name to The Knights of Malta, attained their greatest eminence and power, and became a sovereign Order. The Knights of Malta remained in Malta till Napoleon captured it in 1798 when Ferdinand von Hompseach, the last grand master, resigned. After the British took over the island, the knights moved to Ferrara and then in 1834 moved once again and settled as a very small community in Rome. The badge of the Order is a white and silver 8-pointed star on a black mantle.

The Knights of Malta had priories in eight countries, one of which was England. The English priory was suppressed in 1540, restored in 1557 and finally abolished in 1559. St. John's Gate, Clerkenwell, a relic of the Order's possessions is still standing and is the headquarters of the Order of St. John of Jerusalem, an English foundation incorporated on 14th May 1888.

These three military orders whose roots sprang from the soil of Palestine 800 years ago lost their original purpose after the end of the Crusades. Their task was finished in the flower of their youth and they were an anachronism by the end of the Middle Ages. Born into a world which might have welcomed their presence, they perished in one which had no further use for them.

It is appropriate in a chapter devoted to knighthood to add a brief description of horse armour. The trouble is that the knight's charger was still naked and unashamed in 1326, the year artillery made its appearance. Strictly speaking, therefore, any description of subsequent armour for the horse is beyond the scope of this survey. It is true that prior to the introduction of cannon some forms of horse protection were to be seen, but these were arbitrary, motley and fragmentary. Occasionally, chain mail is seen depicted, sometimes quilted material and at other *cuir-boulli*. Often the chain mail was covered with a light material. When full plate armour for the horse was introduced about 1430, it consisted of:

The *chanfron*, which protected the face. This was often furnished with a spike projecting from the forehead.
The *crinet*, which protected the neck.
The *peytral*, which protected the chest.
The *flanchards*: hanging pieces of plate to protect the flanks.
The *crupper*, which protected the hind-quarters of the horse. This was often provided with a tail-guard.
The *estivals*: metallic casings for the legs. Seldom used.

Horse plate armour was often supplemented by reinforced chain mail, quilted coverings and leather.

CHAPTER IX

MILITARY ORGANISATION AND WEAPONS

There appears to be a sinister pattern running through all systems of military service which mitigates against the success of any organisation built upon its foundations. This pattern, like that of life, is one of growth, fulfilment, decay and ultimate extinction. The key to all military success is the possession of the initiative, i.e. the power of decision; and all countries have had to take this into account when framing their military policies, though in the past lack of mechanical skill and the worldwide similarity of simple weapons forced armies to conform to a mode of combat which allowed little room for manoeuvre. Military organisations therefore tended to be identical. Like the life-span of man there is a uniformity in the birth and death of empires. The emergent state, wishing to play a prominent part in world affairs, is imbued with a strong desire for action. Her young men, inspired by patriotism, flock to the colours and are willing to undergo a tough period of training. In due course, victory having crowned the efforts of her citizens by enlarging her territory and increasing her trade, the tempo slackens. Acquired wealth begets sloth and the demands of commerce tend to quench the fighting spirit. Luxury spreads and the pursuit of pleasure becomes preferable to the discipline of the camp. As a result, the original conscript or militiaman is replaced by the mercenary and the slave. Leaders grow ambitious and rivalry breaking out among them often leads to sectional armies. In these circumstances, an insidious blight descends upon the forces which deteriorate rapidly. Finally, the initiative is lost and the question of defence, the last refuge of a crumbling dynasty, appears more important than that of attack. This process may take generations to complete but the end is certain; the empire collapses, to be replaced by another more virile which in its turn follows the same cycle from strength to weakness. In this manner, the Great Powers parade through the pages of history.

This initiative was originally based on moral and economic grounds, i.e. on the national will to wage a victorious war. As weapons, however, became more complex and the engines of war assumed a greater degree of importance, a modified form called the *technical initiative* marked a new trend. This, obtained by applying engineering skill to matters of attack and defence, may be defined as the ability to develop and maintain without foreign interference or financial restriction a weapon-power technique superior to that of any possible enemy and to evolve a strategic policy accordingly. The war potential of a country is determined by its reserves of manpower, its economic resources and its supplies of raw materials, and the extent to which, and the rapidity with which, these can become militarised, i.e. its *latent* military power. The technical initiative must therefore be acquired and resolutely maintained during peace so that in the event of hostilities it can fructify the war potential and convert latent military power into active armed strength. This policy will always call for courage, imagination and sacrifice but there is no alternative worthy of a moment's thought. The issue is clear: security or insecurity; survival or death. In this light, technical initiative can be described as the link binding the cunning of the engineer to the weapon of the soldier.

Byzantium appears to have been the only empire of the past to have put this philosophy, at least partially, into practice with the result that notwithstanding failing resources, dwindling revenues and loss of territory she managed to retain her suzerainty for 1,100 years till she was finally overthrown by Mahomet II in A.D. 1453.

EGYPT

Ramses II, who ascended the throne of Egypt about 1300 B.C., is said to have formed one of the earliest military organisations in the world. His plan was to divide the country into thirty-six military districts and at the same time create a militia of warriors who were to be allotted lands for the upkeep of themselves and their families. The army, comprising four territorial divisions, was formed of archers and heavy infantrymen. The former, who fought either on foot or in chariots, acted as the wings of the army in action. In addition, there were bodies of cavalry drawn from north Africa. These covered the foot-soldiers and gave them mounted support in battle. The centre consisted of the infantry who were divided into regiments, each distinguished by the particular class of weapon they carried. As well as her own nationals, Egyptian forces included mercenaries from her allies and slaves from conquered lands. The efficiency of such an army depended on the co-operation of the various races comprising it.

In action, the heavy infantry, armed with spears, shields and falchions, moved in close formation in the form of an impregnable phalanx, each company with its own special standard being protected by the archers and the cavalrymen. Troops were summoned by trumpet and this instrument as well as the long drum were employed for this purpose from the dawn of Egyptian history. The soldiers' offensive weapons were the bow, the spear, the sling, the javelin, the sword, the dagger, the knife, the falchion, the axe, the battle-axe, the pole-axe, the mace and the *lissan* or curved throwing stick. Quite an extensive array of equipment for an ancient people. Their defensive armour consisted of a metal helmet or quilted head-piece, a cuirass covered with thin metal plates and a shield. They did not possess greaves and the only protection afforded to their arms was that given by the short sleeves of the cuirass which extended down to the elbow.

THE HITTITES

The Hittites from Cappadocia swarmed over the Middle East and in due course formed the Hittite Empire which about 1300 B.C. began to vie with Egypt for mastery over the countries bordering the Mediterranean. Governors of provinces were in duty bound to provide bodies of men for the national army in time of war. In addition, there was a standing force in permanent garrisons, the veterans of which were rewarded with grants of land. They were the great exponents of the archer-manned chariot. In due course they overran Babylon. Their empire disintegrated about 1000 B.C.

ASSYRIA

'The Assyrian came down like the wolf on the fold
And his cohorts were gleaming in purple and gold'

So wrote Lord Byron in *The Destruction of Sennacherib*. Rather a flattering description perhaps? Who knows? But the Assyrian army cost the royal treasury a substantial annual sum to maintain. It was based on a regular professional force which formed the backbone of its fighting efficiency. These regular soldiers included the king's bodyguard and a special *corps d'élite* which acted as a steadying influence on the auxiliaries drawn from the provinces and on the national militia which could be called up during a state of emergency. This immense body of men was organised on the decimal system; units of 10, 100 or 1,000, etc. Originally, the armed forces consisted only of infantrymen and charioteers, the latter being relatively few in number. The chariots were cumbersome vehicles lacking mobility. They carried two men, a driver and a soldier, usually a bowman. Later on, a lighter chariot was introduced. This was less clumsy in action and had the advantage of carrying a third occupant to shield the archer when firing. Cavalry armed with lances or bows was added in the 9th century B.C. The infantry formed the bulk of the fighting forces. They were armed with the spear, the sword, the sling and the bow. They wore helmets and coats of mail and in addition bore shields. Archers were protected by large shields of wood or wickerwork and during the siege of a city these shields were placed side by side to form a palisade behind which the bowmen could carry on their deadly work under cover. The Assyrians were greatly addicted to the theory of investment. Sieges to them were the acme of tactical success.

BABYLONIA

The Babylonian army consisted of a citizen force mobilised in time of war. By the reign of Hammurabi, however, a corps of professional soldiers had been formed which acted as a centre of picked troops in battle, though the bulk of the armed forces was still recruited on a territorial basis. The soldier wore a helmet and a leather cuirass and carried either a spear, a dagger, a mace or a battle-axe. Besides infantry, a number of chariots accompanied the army into battle. These usually contained an archer or a foot-soldier armed with a lance. Having broken away from Assyria, the Babylonians with the assistance of the Medes crushed the Assyrians at the siege of Nineveh in 612 B.C.

PERSIA

Persia maintained a standing army for garrison duties, the officers of which were Persian. So were the famous 10,000 Immortals. The king's bodyguard was also composed of Persian nationals. Foreign mercenaries were recruited into the Persian forces. This army was organised for battle in massed concentrations of infantry with cavalry concealed in the intervals between the squares. The Persians have always been expert horsemen and their cavalry was at one time the envy of the world. Troops were armed with spears, lances, swords and bows. In times of emergency a national levy was ordered. This resulted in a heterogeneous collection of barbarous and undisciplined hordes with the result that on mobilisation the army's fighting qualities suffered. This defect was responsible in part for the defeat of Mardonius by the Greeks at Plataea in 479 B.C.

In spite of this inherent weakness, however, Persia in biblical times still retained an enormous empire, the like of which the world had never before seen. Despite its ups and downs, its periods of greatness and decline, the Peacock Throne is the only one of the ancient empires which has survived the scourge of war and the ravages of time down to the present day.

CARTHAGE

Carthage, a seaport city devoted to commerce, was first and foremost a maritime power. Her principal strength lay in her powerful fleet which was essential to guard her trade routes as her life-blood depended on seaborne traffic. She was one of the greatest entrepots of the ancient world. Founded some 2,800 years ago she became in due course one of the main rivals of Rome. The Mediterranean was too small to hold two such mighty giants, hence the famous pronouncement of Marcus Porcius Cato *Delenda est Carthago* with which he ended all his speeches in the Senate. This threat was eventually carried out in 146 B.C. when the younger

Complete equipment of Persian horseman.   The man wears a coat of mail, and the horse is covered with an armour composed of plates of iron joined together with small chain links.   From a manuscript in the library of Munich, illustrated with 215 beautiful miniatures, illuminated about the year 1580 to 1600.   It is a copy of the Schah Nameh or Royal Book, a poem composed by Ferdusi, in the reign of Mahmoud the Gaznevide (999).

Fig. 49.—A Persian horseman.

Scipio destroyed the city which stood about twelve miles from the site of modern Tunis.

The principal dockyard was situated in the city and, in addition, there were two havens, an outer one for merchants and an inner one separated from the outer by a double wall. A small island in the inner commanding a view of the sea contained the naval headquarters. Two hundred and twenty ships of the line were normally at anchor in the dockyard, equipped and ready to sail at short notice. These vessels, known as *quinqueremes*, carried 420 men; 120 soldiers and 300 rowers—the latter being slaves specially purchased for this task by the state. The naval command was usually distinct from that of the army though sometimes a generalissimo-in-chief was appointed in war.

The land forces of the republic consisted principally of hired mercenaries since the Carthaginians being engaged in business had little time to indulge in military training. Having the means to purchase their soldiers, they considered the hiring of fighting men an economic bargain. Members of the ruling families, however, did serve in the army and all commanders were drawn from this source. As the military forces of this famous city were a polyglot mixture of humanity, some professional soldiers, some semi-savage and others slaves, it is not really possible to describe the arms they carried nor the protective covering they wore. 'Rabble' may be too strong a word to apply to the Carthaginian army, but it was composed mainly of a mixture of warriors who fought because it was their trade and of ill-trained slaves who had no choice in the matter. Troops of Carthaginian or Phoenician origin formed the centre of the army in battle and the wings consisted of nomadic African tribesmen. Slingers from the Balearic Isles constituted the vanguard and elephants from Ethiopia with their coal-black mahouts, the ancient forerunners of the modern tank, were employed to guard the front line. There was method in obtaining men of various nationalities for the army. It was considered that differences of language would lessen the danger of conspiracy, though it did make inter-communication more difficult. It may be said without exaggeration that the Punic army was an amalgam of the tribes of the western world and the African desert. Such an organisation obviously contained seeds of weakness which germinated in due course leading in the end to total destruction.

To gather some idea of the size of the naval and military forces of Carthage, even in time of peace, it must be remembered that her overseas trading ports were garrisoned and that during the short intervals between wars it was essential to keep in active being an armed force sufficient to meet the hazard of hostilities.

Three hundred elephants, stabling for 4,000 horses, accommodation for their riders and barracks for 40,000 foot-soldiers were always available in the city.

GREECE

The armed forces of Greece consisted of a militia subject to almost continuous training. The discipline was strict, being the fruit of a highly specialised form of moral and physical education. The profession of soldiering was confined to free citizens, slaves being prohibited from bearing arms except on occasions of extreme national peril. Sparta originated the massed formation of foot-soldiers known as the *phalanx*, which was the basis of all Greek military formations. This was successively modified and improved by various states. Athens made it more mobile and added light troops to cover its attacks. Thebes introduced the column to pierce the enemy's line at some point and throw it into confusion. Philip V of Macedon made the phalanx deeper and still more massive. He brought into use the Macedonian pike, a redoubtable weapon 24 feet in length. With a phalanx sixteen feet in depth six rows of men could present the points of these fearsome pikes well in advance of the front rank offering a glittering array of steel frightful to encounter—a veritable 'hedgehog' of the battlefield.

This heavy infantry phalanx formed the main strength of the Greek forces and was for long invincible. The men who composed it wore armour, bore broad shields and carried long spears, afterwards replaced, as has been said, by formidable Macedonian pikes. In addition to this massed infantry formation, there were light troops and cavalry, the latter introduced after the Persian war. The former were drawn from the poorer classes and armed with slings, darts, bows and arrows. They did not seem to play any definite part in battle, their role being more in the nature of a nuisance value to distract the enemy. Having discharged their missiles they usually fell back behind the protecting shields of the heavy infantry. The cavalry was confined to aristocrats who could afford to supply their own mounts. Their numbers, therefore, were never large. Some consisted of mounted archers and slingers who could be considered light troopers; others formed the heavy horse. Cavalrymen also fought in chariots and under Alexander the Great on elephants. The charioteers were normally members of the nobility. Their chariots were of the usual type. The crew

Fig. 59.—Grecian armour.

consisted of two men, the driver and the warrior, the latter being the commander who gave instructions to the former. The fighting man was clad in a leather cuirass and a helmet, and carried a spear and a large circular shield.

Elephants as mounts for heavy cavalrymen were introduced by

Alexander the Great, but owing to the difficulty of controlling the great beasts when wounded their use was soon abandoned. Their presence did of course offer advantages, both moral and physical, but their sensitiveness on the battlefield outweighed their usefulness. Over 2,000 years later, elephant batteries in India were discontinued for the same reason even though the Asian elephant was always more docile and amenable than his African cousin.

The heavy cavalry, formed into regiments distinguishable by their armour, were either lancers, swordsmen or javelin throwers; in later times the protection of armour was extended to their horses. Alexander the Great also instituted a kind of mounted infantry. These men being heavily armed could dismount, hand their horses over to attendants and fight alongside the infantry proper. There appears to be no evidence that cavalry were ever used for reconnaissance, which in modern times became such an important part of its functions.

Plutarch tells us that Philomenes, master of the Achaean horse, paid particular attention to the Greek cavalry and tried to remedy its faults. He ordered them to carry a light shield and use much shorter lances, which owing to their lesser weight could be hurled at the enemy and yet at the same time be robust enough to engage in armed conflict. In this way he hoped to train his forces to act is a dual capacity, either to skirmish as light horse or to sustain a charge from heavy cavalry. In like manner, Philoemen, a distinguished general of the Achaean league, persuaded his infantrymen to cover their bodies with breastplates and their legs with greaves and to use Argolic shields and long spears in place of the short spears and oblong shields which they formerly handled.

The Neolithic Greek warrior clad himself in animal skins, chiefly those of dogs, and wore a headpiece of bull's hide. These coats of skin were always worn hair outwards to magnify the ferocious appearance of the wearer. Often the dead animal's teeth were arranged in a ghastly grin to intensify the horror aspect, a custom adopted by the early Mexicans. Later, the Homeric Greeks used bronze arms and armour, and as time passed the latter was often richly ornamented and the helmets adorned with plumes of feathers. Greek armour during the passage of centuries developed *pari passu* with that of other countries. They possessed several types of shield, the shapes of which were governed by the uses to which they were to be put. To lose a shield in battle was considered to be a shameful disgrace.

For close fighting the soldiers used clubs, spears, lances, maces, battle-axes, pole-axes, swords and daggers but the club soon disappeared in favour of the mace. The spear was generally of ash with a leaf-shaped metal head shod with a pointed ferrule. The Macedonians employed a particularly long spear some 21 to 24 feet in length. The lance was furnished with a loop of leather to act as a support when the lancer hung it on his arm and as a grip improver when used in the charge. The swords differed in shape; some straight for thrusting and others curved for cutting and slashing. The sling followed normal design and the bow was made from two long goat's horns fitted with a handle in the middle. The original bowstrings were thongs of leather but afterwards horsehair was substituted. The arrows, normally carried in a quiver, had pointed heads, sometimes pyramidal in shape, and their shafts were furnished with feathers.

ROME

The Romans in their finest hour had one of the best armies in the ancient world. They were by nature a nation of warriors who took the security and advancement of their homeland seriously. Every citizen was obliged to enlist when public duty called, and so important was service in the armed forces considered that no one could enjoy office unless he had at least ten campaigns to his credit. About 200 B.C. every male inhabitant of Rome between the ages of 17 and 46 was liable to be called to the colours and although the younger men were preferred those of a more mature age could be drafted if required. The training was thorough and the discipline severe in order to fit the new recruits for the rigours of campaigning. The instruction included drill, marching, the art of combat, camping and other duties of a military nature. Every year magistrates forwarded lists of men eligible for enlistment to the tribunes who selected the numbers required to keep the legions up to establishment. The Roman legion retained its militia character till Augustus established permanent forces on the frontiers and armies of occupation for vanquished territories. The Roman army was in many respects like that of Great Britain in its great colonial days except that England normally relied on voluntary enlistment. When Rome withdrew her legions from her dependencies the Dark Ages followed and at the present time European countries appear to be carrying out an identical policy with somewhat similar results.

The Roman army in its heyday was organised in legions, each consisting of ten cohorts of infantry, ten troops of cavalry and the legionary 'artillery'. The cohort contained three maniples consisting two centuries each. It was nominally 600 strong though its numbers varied with the strength of the legion, which depended on its tasks, but whatever the infantry complement of a legion the cohort formed a tenth part of it.

Each century of foot-soldiers had its own standard and standard bearer. This was originally a bundle of hay lashed to a pole but in succeeding years this was replaced by a spear with a cross-piece of wood on the top bearing above the representation of a hand and below an oval shield usually of silver or gold. Standards of the different divisions of the legion had certain letters inscribed on them as a distinguishing sign. The legion's standard was a silver eagle with outstretched wings, sometimes grasping a thunderbolt in its claws. This standard was located near the general commanding almost in the centre of the legion. The centurion in charge of the first century of the first maniple of the first cohort was charged with guarding the legion's standard—a most responsible post— and thus the first cohort was granted precedence over the other nine.

The legion's foot was divided into heavy and light infantry. The former comprised the *hastati*, the *principes* and the *triarii*, and the latter the *velites*, the *funditores* and the *sagittarii*. The *hastati* earned their name because they fought originally with *hastae* or long spears and at that time formed the centre rank being able to reach beyond those of the front line. As, however, they consisted of young men in the flower of their youth, they were afterwards promoted to the front rank and discarded their long spears. The normal Roman spear was just over six feet in length and was carried by both officers and men. The *principes* were men of middle age who derived their name from having originally fought in the front rank; afterwards, however, they were demoted to the second rank. One of these of the first cohort actually carried the standard of the legion in battle. The *triarii* were the veterans, old soldiers of proved valour who formed the third line. They were armed with the *pilum* or short spear.

The armour of the three classes of heavy infantry was very similar. The *scutum* or oblong shield, the round buckler, a head-piece of brass or iron called a *cassis* or a *galea* made of leather. In later times both terms were applied indifferently. The body armour was the *lorica* or leathern corselet which was afterwards fashioned from brass. The laminated *lorica* which eventually superseded the earlier pattern was a very heavy piece of equipment and its weight at the time of the Emperor Galba (A.D. 68) was made the subject of a complaint by the legionaries. The original corselets of the *triarii*, however, appear to have been made only of leather. By the time of Marcus Aurelius (A.D. 161–180) the oblong shield had given way to the round brazen shield (*clypeus*) and the *triarii* were clad in a cuirass of iron scales. The *clypeus* itself was laid aside in the time of Constantine (A.D. 306–337) when the hexagonal shield was adopted. In the days of the republic Roman soldiers were bare-legged like the highlander but during the empire they wore pantaloons which reached down to the calves of their legs. They were shod with *caligae*, a kind of sandal having spikes underneath like the running shoes of the modern athlete. The Emperor Caligula earned his name from wearing this form of footgear. Roman officers wore a military cloak of scarlet edged with purple. This was worn over the tunic of *sagum*, a coarse woollen mantle said to have been borrowed from the Gauls.

The light infantry, called collectively *ferentarii* or *rorarii* (skirmishers) were also as before stated sub-divided into three classes. The *velites*, so-called from their mobility, were introduced during the Second Punic War (218–201 B.C.). They had no armour except a helmet and a round shield three feet in diameter (*parma*) made of wood and covered with leather. Each man carried seven javelins. These had a wooden shaft 3 feet long and 1 inch thick to which was attached a steel blade six inches in length with so fine a point that it became blunted on first impact thus preventing it from being hurled back by the enemy. The *funditores* or slingers hailed either from the Balearic Isles or Achaea. The *sagittarii* or archers were of different nationalities though many came from Crete or Arabia. The arrows they used were not only barbed but, in addition, were furnished with hooks just above the points to

Fig. 51.—Roman armour.

make extraction from flesh extremely difficult. All these classes of light troops wore a *galerum* or bonnet made from the skins of wild beasts in place of the *galea* or leather helmet, in order to increase the savagery of their appearance.

The Roman cavalry, who used spurs and bits but had neither stirrups nor saddles, originally wore their own garments for the sake of agility in mounting. The saddle was adopted later during the reign of Theodosius I (A.D. 379–95). Polybius, describing the cavalry of about 150 B.C., says that the armour then worn by them was similar to that donned by the Greeks. They did not formerly wear corselets but only had coverings for the thighs. This undoubtedly added to their mobility but at the same time exposed them to greater danger. He points out that their javelins were useless as they were too light except for a single thrust, and that the shields they carried were not proof against penetration. He goes on to say that after the submission of Greece in 147 B.C. the Roman cavalry discarded their previous equipment and adopted that of the Greeks.

The *equites cataphracti* or heavy cavalry were a later innovation in the legion, being introduced about the time of Constantine the Great. They and their horses were clad in steel, the men wearing breastplates girt with iron bands. Ammianus Marcellinus says that they were similar to the Persian *clibanarii*. Vegetius disapproved strongly of this kind of heavy cavalry. He says 'The *equites cataphracti* are free from the likelihood of wounds owing to the armour they wear, but its inconvenience and weight render them more liable to capture'. Josephus described the Greek cavalry in the service of Rome during the destruction of Jerusalem as having a long sword at their right side, a long *contus* in their hand, three or four javelins in a quiver and a heavy spear.

The legion's 'artillery' consisted of catapults and *carro-balistae*, the latter being *balistae* on wheels harnessed to mules so arranged as to discharge their missiles over the heads of the draught animals. Every cohort was equipped with a catapult drawn on a heavy cart yoked to oxen and every century had one *carro-balista* with a detachment of eleven men. Thus 60 *carro-balistae* and 10 catapults accompanied the legion into action.

Totting up the figures of the various arms this gives a total of about 7,000 men as the war establishment of a large legion. This body bore a striking resemblance to the British division.

To enforce discipline, a centurion was detailed to see that all equipment used by the infantry was properly maintained, and a decurion—the commander of a *decuria* or troop of horse—to oversee the cavalry and assure himself that their weapons and mounts were kept in good order.

In cities bodies of soldiers were employed under a prefect as watchmen, one cohort being supplied for every two wards. Such men could be equated with modern military police. These individuals, chiefly manumitted slaves, wore over their tunics three leather straps which crossed longitudinally in front and behind. At the intersection of these straps hung a bell.

During the first two centuries of Christendom the character of the Roman people and their army changed. Insurrections broke out at home and place-seekers strove for the highest fruits of office. In the space of sixty years no less than sixteen emperors and more than thirty would-be emperors perished by violence. External strife also threatened the empire, for the barbarians beyond the pale were getting more venturesome. But in A.D. 250 the legion was still a heavily armed infantry formation, the mainstay of the battle and the hope of the commander. It had, however, the smell of death in its nostrils and was becoming a pale counterpart of its former self. In another two centuries it had virtually disappeared, its place being taken by the mounted soldier who had thrust his comrade on foot into the background; so much so that by the time of the Emperor Valens the word 'legion' had almost passed from the memory of the Roman citizen. The old-time military effectiveness based on strength and flexibility, solid yet easy to command, had ceased to cater for the needs of the period and was doomed to extinction. The sword and the *pilum* had retreated before the lance and the bow. The Roman soldier of the 5th century A.D. was no longer the ironclad legionary who hurled defiance at his foes and stood unmoved before the advance of savage hordes. The old military organisation of the Caesars began to crumble in the 3rd century; in the 4th it was so transformed and weakened as to be almost unrecognisable; by the end of the 5th it lay in ruins.

The replacement of the legion by cavalry and light infantry, immobility versus movement, the bow and lance in place of the heavy spear took place mainly as a result of border troubles. The enemies who now faced Rome were in the main natural horsemen who had been trained to the saddle from birth. They were swift nomadic antagonists not cumbersome men confined in massed formations. The character of tactics was changing from the pitched battle of the strongly held position to the open warfare of the plains. To compete with this situation the Roman military command between A.D. 120 and 210 adopted a system of frontier defence round the periphery of the empire using natural objects, such as rivers, mountains, etc. as far as possible. In exposed places they built walls or extensive ditches and covered these with permanent forts often hundreds of miles apart. These were garrisoned by legionaries, but the long distances between these encampments were filled with minor stations housing a few auxiliaries who patrolled the undefended perimeter. This was indeed a policy of despair, the surrender of initiative, relying on defence rather than on attack. This strategic conception stabilised matters for a hundred years but it had its weakness. It lacked a strong central reserve from which troops could be rushed to guard a threatened point, because the inner provinces behind the defended line were kept denuded of troops and new legions, owing to the unwillingness of citizens to come forward, were difficult to raise. Thus to prevent an incursion, troops had to be moved from another frontier area, and moved quickly, to expel the prospective invader, a highly dangerous procedure when foes were massing on all sides and might be expected to attack in several places simultaneously. Interior lines do offer advantages but not when troops are too thinly spread on the ground. This system naturally broke down when enemies attacked in force from several directions at once.

As a result of stupendous advances by the Goths, Rome was well nigh overwhelmed. But the end was not yet. Claudius, Aurelian, Probus and Diocletian saved the situation by reconquering most of the lost provinces so that on the map the empire resumed its old shape. After twenty years of labour Diocletian restored a semblance of public order and internal strength. By imposing enormous taxes he replenished the imperial exchequer and was able to repair the broken-down frontier of the Roman world. He abolished the age-old distinction between the legionary who was a Roman citizen and an auxiliary who was not. He created an Imperial guard and a great number of new units who were 'colonial'. They were made into a huge reserve imperial army, distinct from the legionary defence of the frontier, and it could be moved anywhere it was needed without weakening the frontier defence forces.

Constantine, too, made many changes with a view to restoring the old invincible Roman army. This restoration, sound on paper, was only skin-deep in reality. Underneath the façade, internal struggles, anarchy, sloth and luxurious living played their insidious parts in sapping the strength of the country and ruining the morale of the army. The legion became more and more moribund and cavalry more and more the chosen arm, till the former as a military body disappeared. The decline and ultimate decay of the once all-powerful empire is too long a story to tell but its outline provides a fitting reminder of the impermanence of all things temporal. By A.D. 400 the days of heavy infantry in southern Europe were numbered and as a decisive factor in war it soon ceased to exist. In A.D. 410 the decisive battle took place which sealed the fate of the old Roman Empire; on 24th August of that year Alaric and his followers advanced on Rome, sacked the city and obliterated all traces of the invincible Roman army.

BYZANTIUM

The Byzantines were not particularly warlike in character. They were first and foremost a nation of traders, engineers and artists who preferred to pursue the arts of peace. Martial glory was something quite alien to their nature. They realised of course that, the world being as it was, the soldier was a necessary adjunct to society and, as such, had his allotted place, but he never shared the glory of his western brother. The diplomat's object was to avoid bloodshed at all costs and the profession of diplomacy was considered to be quite as important as that of arms. But, regretfully perhaps, the authorities at Byzantium did realise that their exposed position in an unsettled corner of the Middle East did warrant the maintenance of strong naval and military forces if their way of life was to remain undisturbed. The Byzantine army, therefore, if not the equal of that of imperial Rome, was an efficient force of often outstanding quality. Service in the armed forces was originally obligatory and veterans were rewarded with grants of land in Asia Minor.

The art of war, strangely enough, had always been an object of study in Byzantium and she had produced many notable writers on the subject; whereas in Europe military training had been regarded primarily as a question of tough fighting. The young Frankish nobleman deemed his education complete when he could sit his horse and handle his weapon with skill; his Byzantine counterpart on the other hand, quite as well trained in the use of arms, added theory to practice by studying his country's text-books. He therefore made a worthy antagonist. Since Byzantium fostered among other things the study of engineering, she employed many of her citizens in what would now be termed scientific research. The knowledge thus acquired was applied to the study of war and so Byzantium secured a technical initiative which stood her in good stead for so many years.

The old legionary system disappeared about A.D. 380 having been replaced by the *foederati* (light cavalry) founded by Theodosius I A.D. 379–95). These consisted of barbarian regiments or even whole tribes who took service with the Romans under the leadership of their princes. This operation was not a success as the barbarians became a law unto themselves. Leo I (A.D. 457–74), however, was able to check their excesses and by the following century the *foederati* were brought under control. Under Theodosius I, the army was divided into two commands, one a *theme* consisting of local men recruited on a part-time basis who remained settled in their own localities, the other a mobile expeditionary force of mercenaries capable of taking the field at short notice. The best troops came from Illyria, Isauria and Thrace; the mercenaries being Huns, Herulians and later Langobardians. The latter served as mounted scouts but they were less reliable than the regular cavalry who consisted of the *foederati* and the *caballarii* (heavy troopers). The former were very lightly armoured and armed mainly with the bow. The latter wore a cap surmounted by a small tuft, a long shirt of mail, gauntlets and steel shoes. All rode on saddles with large iron stirrups. The heavy trooper was supplied with a light linen surcoat to put over his armour in hot weather and a large woollen overcoat for cold and rainy days. Each *banda* (band), consisting of three to four hundred men, had its own particular colour for its tufts, lance-pennons and surcoats. The army therefore wore a definite uniform. It was the cavalryman's bow which proved so deadly in battle. Its introduction gave a measure of flexibility to an otherwise cumbrous formation and played a decisive part in winning victories. Time and again it was concentrated arrow-fire which put an enemy to flight before he had had time to consolidate his position. In addition to the regular army, certain generals maintained their own guard regiments who, armed with swords and bows, were well trained and faithful to their masters. The private army of Belisarius is said to have numbered 7,000 men.

The strength of the East Roman army between A.D. 580 and 912 lay in its heavy cavalry, the infantry playing a minor role connected with frontier defence and garrison duties. The infantry were also divided into light and heavy regiments. The light infantryman was chiefly armed with the bow though some preferred the javelin. The archer carried forty arrows and a small round buckler slung on his back. The heavy foot-soldier was clad in a pointed helmet carrying a tuft on top, a mail shirt, gauntlets and greaves. He bore a large round shield, a lance, a sword and a battle-axe having a cutting blade on one side and a spike on the other. Like the cavalry, the colour of the helmet tuft and the shield was uniform throughout the band.

After the loss of Syria and Palestine to the Arabs in the 7th century, the whole defensive system was again changed and it was then that the idea of settling residential forces along the borders of Asia Minor was fully developed. This was, in fact, a repetition of the frontier defence policy of Rome in the 2nd century thus again abandoning the initiative. The conquest of this area by the Seljuks in the 11th century brought this defensive system crashing to the ground. After that disaster taxes were levied in lieu of service, a policy which weakened both the size and morale of the land forces to such an extent that eventually the country had to rely almost entirely on mercenary troops.

Both cavalry and infantry in the field were followed by a large baggage train. For every sixteen men there was a ration cart carrying food and spare arrows; and a stores vehicle containing stores, cooking utensils and entrenching tools. In addition, a pack-horse to carry iron rations for eight or ten men accompanied the waggons. A corps of engineers marched with the vanguard and and ambulance detachment consisting of an apothecary, a surgeon and six to eight stretcher-bearers formed part of the organisation. The stretcher bearers were furnished with a large flagon of water and horses for transporting the wounded.

Cavalry tactics were much more elaborate than those for the infantry. Battle tactics for the imperial cavalry laid down that the force must be divided into:

(1) A front line: three-eighths of the whole force.
(2) A supporting line: one-third of the whole force.
(3) A small reserve behind the supporting line: about one-tenth of the whole force.
(4) Flank guards to protect the main body or turn the enemy's flanks: one-fifth of the whole force.

The *banda* was commanded by a *comes* or a tribune, a number of *bandae* formed a *moira* or brigade commanded by a *moerarchus* or *dux*. In cavalry formations, the brigade was called a *drungus* and was commanded by a *drungarius*. Two or more brigades formed a *turma* or division. The proportions and complements of these units were intentionally kept vague in order to confuse the enemy. The grouping of bands after a declaration of war was the responsibility of the commander-in-chief.

Although an army was essential to Byzantium, the navy played an equally important role though it was never granted the same status as its sister service. Byzantium with its virtual command of the Mediterranean till about A.D. 700 had built up an enormous trade and became the great entrepot between east and west, a position which Carthage had held almost 1,000 years before. In the great days of the empire when the Mediterranean was a Roman lake there was little need for a large fleet. Byzantium was quite capable of checking the activities of Black Sea pirates with a small complement of ships. Even when the Goths ravaged southern Europe a limited number of ships had been sufficient to blockade the coast and make the barbarians move on. It was only when the Vandals arrived in Africa and amassed a fleet that the inadequacy of the Eastern Empire's naval plans became apparent. Little heed, however, was paid to the warning until the growing Arab sea-power menaced Byzantium and made her aware of the danger she faced. So when the *themes* were being founded, two naval *themes* were included, with admirals instead of generals as governors. These were known as the *Cibyrrhaeot* covering the southern coast of Asia Minor and the *Aegean* made up of the islands and parts of the western coast of the same area. Each *theme* was commanded by a *drungarius* and both drungarii were under the supreme command of the *strategus* of the *carabisiani*. The warship favoured by the Byzantines was the *dromond*, a *bireme* holding between 100 and 300 men. In addition, they had swifter biremes known as *pamphylians* and a certain number of single-tiered small galleys. The ships were armed with battering rams and syphons which projected Greek fire. This flame-throwing equipment, the main form of naval armament, was responsible for many Byzantine victories at sea.

A strong maritime organization having been built up it became in time too powerful politically and dethroned a couple of emperors. The civic authorities, duly alarmed, proceeded to curtail the navy's power and reduce the number of its ships, a step deemed safe as Arab sea-power appeared to be on the wane. This proved to be an untimely measure for which the seaport city had to pay dearly. In due course Arab naval strength re-blossomed and captured Sicily and Crete about A.D. 825. These captures crippled the strength of Byzantium to a certain extent and she lost more of her hold on the southern Mediterranean though she still retained her power in the north.

After this disaster the naval forces of Byzantium were re-organized and strengthened. Crete was recaptured in A.D. 961 and thereafter Arab sea-power dwindled away. Conditions in the Eastern Empire improved and trade expanded so that Constantine VII could truthfully boast that he ruled the waves between the coast of Asia Minor and the Pillars of Hercules. The threat removed, the fleet was again reduced in size. This was due partly to the recurring fear of political dominance, partly to lack of money and mainly to the pressure of statesmen who argued that it was a waste of public money to retain a large fleet when the Arab menace had disappeared.

As the 11th century wore on, the precarious position of the central government made itself more and more felt and the scarcity of funds made retrenchment essential. The fleet was further reduced, the army deteriorated and the coming shadow of defeat darkened the horizon. Four more centuries were to elapse before its final doom overtook the dying empire but these brought further wrangles and decline. Thus in the end the little Greek community founded at Byzantium in 657 B.C., re-created as Constantinople by Constantine the Great on 11th May A.D. 333 and forming in due course one of the greatest civilising bastions of the Middle Ages succumbed, not to the Arabs but to the Turks, their erstwhile mercenaries. On that fateful day, 29th May 1453, a great Christian state, the seat of the Orthodox Church, vanished under the onslaught of the infidel marching under the banner of the Crescent.

ARABIA

The Arab Empire was not an empire in the strict sense of the word; it was more in the nature of an invasion. The word *empire* is usually taken to mean a state, which having conquered surrounding territories by force of arms, blossoms into a large community of diverse peoples governed from the capital of that state. The Arabs, however, were not a nation. They were a confederation of warlike tribes moved by a common religion who started their incursions under the banner of Mahomet. Beginning in a small way at Medina, the sons of the Prophet advanced beyond their narrow borders and swept like a tidal wave over most of the civilised world. The stream started at the beginning of the 7th century and developing into a flood captured country after country till by the middle of the 9th century the Arabs controlled an area stretching from central Asia to the Atlantic seaboard. The Arabs never subdued Byzantium which stood alone surrounded by an infidel world, but they swallowed up Persia, Afghanistan, parts of central Asia and India, Egypt, Syria, the Middle East, the North African littoral and eventually Spain. It was an amazing expansion in so short a time. Then the tide receded and decline set in. Jealousy, anarchy and treachery reared their heads, mercenaries revolted and the Arabian sun set over its vast domains. The Arab conquests left behind them a great heritage of learning, architecture, science, medicine and the arts which had a profound effect upon the Middle Ages. A tornado, similar to that of Genghiz Khan rather than a steady consolidation of power, it blew itself out in a comparatively short space of time. By A.D. 1000 it was a spent force. The troops who fomented this Muslim scourge had no common form of military organisation and are therefore omitted from this chapter.

CHAPTER X

THE RHYTHM OF STRATEGY

The countries bordering the eastern Mediterranean having foot-soldiers armed with short swords, spears and shields reigned supreme on the battlefield during the Bronze Age. They had, it was true, a limited number of horsemen and chariots to assist them but these had small effect on the massed infantrymen who formed the spearhead of attack and the core of defence. The powerful Egyptian phalanx may be taken to illustrate this military formation. The wheel, on which the chariot depended, was invented during the same Age by some unknown genius who conceived the idea of cutting off solid discs from a tree trunk to obtain a wheeled conveyance. In due course, others applied their minds to the problem and evolved the open wheel consisting of a rim, spokes and a nave. This new development added greatly to its potentialities by reducing weight and increasing mobility. This was very noticeable in the chariot which was the first application of the wheel to war.

The Hittites, a people of uncertain origin who conquered much of Asia about 2000 B.C., adopted the wheel and developed it to the best of their ability. They appreciated the advantages it would bestow in the military sphere and decided to improve their fighting efficiency by creating a large number of chariots manned by bowmen in place of the massed infantry formations used by other powers. About 1350 B.C. they overran Egypt, proving that chariot-borne archers could dominate the field.

The chariot with its bowman remained for 900 years the most powerful factor in battle till 22nd September 479 B.C. when the charioteer and his companion were overthrown at Plataea, where 111,000 Greeks under Pausanias overwhelmed 300,000 Persians under Mardonius, leaving 200,000 dead including their commander on the field. For some 300 years the Greek phalanx, improved by Philip V of Macedon, regained the crown for the infantryman in mass but its supremacy was ended by the Roman legions under Mummius when Rome annexed Greece in 146 B.C.

With the exit of Greece and the departure of the phalanx, the Roman legion became the most famous fighting unit in the world. Thus within a short space of time the bowman, the spearman, the chariot and the phalanx had all been swept into oblivion. For 400 years the legion wore a halo of glory but a cloud no bigger than a man's hand was appearing over northern Europe and growing at ominous speed. Beginning about A.D. 200 successive waves of barbarians swept down over southern parts of the continent. These were the Vandals and the Goths.

The Vandals, emanating from Scandinavia, settled at the mouth of the Oder in the first century A.D. and took possession of Silesia and Moravia during the next hundred years. In the 3rd century they broke up into two groups, the Silingians and the Asdingians. The latter acquired their horsemanship from the Sarmatians and lived on the proceeds of their numerous forays, being a restless people who adopted raiding as a way of life. When the Huns appeared in Europe, the two branches of the Vandal family united and attacked Gaul. Driven on by lust of conquest they crossed the frozen Rhine near Mainz on 31st December 406. After three years of spoliation and destruction they passed over into Spain in A.D. 409 and two years later the Emperor Honorius, making a pact with them, admitted them as *foederati* in the Roman forces. This turned out to be a useless gesture for in A.D. 419 they left Galicia and marched south capturing most of the Iberian peninsula and the Roman fleet in A.D. 425. Spurred on by ceaseless ambition they crossed the Straits of Gibraltar in A.D. 429 and made themselves masters of North Africa thereby overrunning the Roman granaries. As a result, Rome had to re-recognise the Vandals as *foederati* and cede them Numidia. Not satisfied with this bribe, and having in the meantime gained command of the Mediterranean, they set sail for Italy in A.D. 455 and in June of that year sacked Rome. After this triumph, dissensions and jealousies broke out among the various factions which raged for the next hundred years till the Vandal kingdom was finally overthrown and their power broken in A.D. 553 by Belisarius who proceeded to make northern Africa a Byzantine province. The Vandals were essentially land pirates and marauders rather than soldiers and their name has survived to this day as a term of infamy. Their irruption had little effect on strategy.

The Goths, who also hailed from Scandinavia, originated in the Swedish province of Gotland. By the second century A.D. they were settled on the lower Vistula. From there they moved into the Ukraine and in A.D. 214 attacked the Romans north of the Danube. Subsequently, they invaded Moesia, the Black Sea area, the Bosphorus, the Dardanelles and the Greek archipelago. By the middle of the 4th century their lands embraced much of present Russia, the Balkans and parts of Turkey. The Goths were divided into two groups, the Visigoths and the Ostrogoths, but when their vast possessions were disrupted by the Huns in A.D. 363 the two branches went their separate ways.

The peregrinations of the Goths are too complicated to be told in a few lines; suffice it to say that the Visigoths, a starving horde of 70,000 souls after their defeat by the Huns, crossed the Danube and sought refuge in Byzantium. At first the East Romans were able to keep these nomadic horsemen in check but in A.D. 378 the pressure grew too great and the Emperor Valens attacked them without waiting for support from the west. The result was disastrous: at the battle of Adrianople on 9th August A.D. 378 the Gothic cavalry routed the Roman infantry killing the emperor himself, many of his senior officials and 40,000 men. The battle broke decisively the power of the Roman legion and proved once again that well-trained, well-disciplined and well-armed cavalry could liquidate the foot-soldier on the battlefield.

The battle of Adrianople was not the end of the Roman Empire but it was the swansong of the Roman legion. Henceforward infantrymen played a minor role in the army, being replaced in the main by heavy cavalry; and to obtain such replacements the Roman command had to depend on the Vandals and the Goths as *foederati* with not always conspicuous success. The unconquered ally is not always subservient to his paymaster. The Goths rode powerful horses and were protected by long shields, helmets and shirts of mail. They were armed with long iron-tipped lances, axes, maces and long cut-and-thrust swords. They rode down their enemy rather than tried to incapacitate him from a distance by the bow. Not only were the Goths magnificent riders, but they

used the stirrup which as much as anything helped them to deci-
mate the Roman troops.

On 3rd October A.D. 382 the Visigoths were recognised as *foederati*. However, they were not content to play second fiddle in a
Roman orchestra. They felt themselves too powerful for subord-
ination. They therefore continued to grow in strength and flow
like a tide over Europe. Greece, Italy and Spain were invaded till
eventually in A.D. 476 their dominion extended from the Straits of
Gibraltar to the Loire, and from the Atlantic to the Alps. Alaric
sacked Rome and entered the starved and strickened city on
24th August A.D. 410. For the first time in eight centuries the
Eternal City was in the hands of an alien power which systemati-
cally pillaged it for three days. Subsequently, owing to defeats in
various engagements, the Visigothic kingdom was confined almost
exclusively to Spain. Even here weaknesses crept in and after a
further two centuries the kingdom fell to the Arabs who crossed
the Straits of Gibraltar in force. At the battle of Cadiz on 19th
July A.D. 711 Spain passed into the hands of its Muslim conquerors
and the Visigoths crumbled into dust.

The Ostrogoths, after their defeat by the Huns, carried out a
similar policy in eastern Europe to that of their distant relatives in
the west. They overran Macedonia, Thrace and parts of the
Balkans. In the autumn of A.D. 488 they moved from Sistova to
Italy. After making themselves masters of that country in A.D. 493
their power gradually waned and was exterminated in A.D. 562
without leaving a trace. With their disappearance their influence
vanished; Gothic prisoners were sold in the slave markets of the
east and the few survivors were absorbed by the Roman population. They were outlived some 150 years by the Visigoths.

While the Goths were invading Europe from the north another
threat was developing from the east. This was caused by a nation
of light cavalry of Asiatic origin called the Huns, who swept like a
whirlwind over Europe. The Huns, a Turco-Mongol people, can
be identified with the Hiung-Lu who by the beginning of the
2nd century A.D. had advanced from Mongolia to the Great Wall
of China and conquered territories between Lake Aral, the north
of the Caspian Sea and the southern Urals. In the 4th century they
set up a puppet state in northern China which collapsed in A.D.

349. In A.D. 363 they spread from the shores of the Caspian to the west thereby precipitating the great Teutonic invasions of the Roman Empire. The Alans, settled between the Caucasus, the Urals and the Don, received the first onslaught and were swept on in the overwhelming rush. Some years later the Huns forced the Don and threw themselves on the Ostrogoths whose resistance was broken about A.D. 376, and the latter's retreat across the Dniester forced the Visigoths to seek shelter in Byzantium. Subsequently, the Huns occupied the Ukraine, Rumania and, in A.D. 406, parts of Hungary.

By the beginning of the 5th century the Hunnish conquests stretched from the eastern Alps to the Urals. During the next few decades under the influence of the subjected Germanic peoples and their contacts with the Roman Empire, an organised Hunnish State was proclaimed and unity of command was established by Attila. By A.D. 448, the Huns began to settle down, desert their nomadic life and live in wooden houses. Although pillage remained their chief occupation, they did assume a veneer of civilisation and maintained commercial relations with Byzantium. They were also in regular communication with the authorities at Ravenna, and Hunnish horsemen took service in the Roman armies. Although the Roman Empire had to pay dearly for this uneasy truce by increasing their concessions time and again it was a sop to fortune which failed. In A.D. 447 the Huns broke off their relations with their Roman paymasters and invaded the Balkans as far as Thermopylae. Peace was restored in A.D. 448 by Byzantium granting large sums of money and ceding provinces between the Danube and the Balkans. Then Attila, kept well-informed by his spies on the parlous state of various principalities, flung his hordes against the west.

The Huns, a novel type of horseman to face Europeans, were a formidable enemy to encounter by virtue of their numbers, their rapidity of movement and their capability of delivering vast quantities of arrows on their foes without allowing the latter to close. In tactics, they were the forerunners of the troops of Alp Arslan, Genghiz Khan and Tamburlane. The influence of the Huns on the Roman army was most marked and profiting by their example the Roman horseman added the bow to his equipment. Thus by the 5th century the native forces of the empire resembled those of Parthia in the 1st century, the best corps being composed of cavalry in mail armed with the bow and lance mixed with mounted archers. It was such forces which fought the German *foederati* armed with the lance alone. These were the troops of Aetius and Ricimer which eventually faced the Huns on the plain of Chalons.

The Huns crossed the Rhine in the spring of A.D. 451 and devastated north-east Gaul as far as the Loire. The Roman commander, Aetius, with an army composed mainly of Visigoths, halted the Huns at the outskirts of Orleans and drove them back, and on 14th June A.D. 451 defeated them on the Muriac Plain near Chalons. After losing this battle, the Huns beat an orderly retreat and invaded Italy in A.D. 452 where they took Aquileia and advanced on Pavia. The Roman government at Ravenna hastened to negotiate but Attila's unexpected death in A.D. 453 when he was about to attack the east cut short the Hunnish success and spelt collapse for the Hunnish empire. None of Attila's sons equalled his father in martial qualities and none could establish authority over the turbulent Asiatic tribesmen. One man's meat is another man's poison and the Germanic peoples, subdued but not crushed, rose in A.D. 454 and chased the Huns back towards the lower Danube and the Black Sea littoral. East of the Dnieper their roving multitudes formed two independent states: the Utrigur Huns between the Dnieper and the Don and the Sabires between the Don, the Caucasus and the Caspian Sea. The former under Dengzic, one of Attila's sons, continued to harass Thrace till the death of their chief in A.D. 468. Thereafter they kept quiet till A.D. 481 when re-inforced by further contingents from Asia they began, under the name of Bulgars, to be a perpetual menace to the Byzantine Empire.

As a result of both these types of invading forces, strategy was for a long time based on a mixture of Gothic and Hunnish methods, but eventually the heavily armed horseman became the dominant figure and developed into the feudal knight whose armour grew more irksome as the years wore on. Another lesson was learned during the Crusades when it was discovered that the Saracens had lighter and more effective chain mail, better swords and deadlier archers. The result of this was that European armourers increased the strength and therefore the weight of the knight's armour thereby making him less mobile.

The last great invasion from the east prior to the discovery of gunpowder was that of Genghiz Khan and his golden horde. Born in A.D. 1154, Genghiz Khan succeeded to a sub-chieftainship of a small Mongolian tribe. He spent forty years in fighting to make himself sole leader of his race. Having accomplished this mission he turned his attention when no longer young to campaigning on such a scale as to ruin many an ancient State. Dr. Edward Kenealy[1] in his work *The Book of God* maintains that Genghiz Khan was one of the seven messengers of God who, in the guise of Destroyer, was sent to purge the world of evil. Whether that claim be true or false, Genghiz Khan was certainly no half-hearted destroyer; Cromwell's treatment of Ireland was in comparison a Sunday school outing. He subjugated Manchuria, northern China, Turkestan and made an end of all the old Muslim principalities on the Oxus. Sweeping over Khiva, Bokhara, Samarkand and the Merv country, he left deserts as his hallmark wherever he went. The golden horde poured over Persia, Mesopotamia and Asia Minor in a ceaseless flood devastating all they came across.

The Tartars first crossed into Europe in A.D. 1224 when Genghiz was 70 years old. One of his armies swept round the south side of the Caspian Sea and after ravaging Azerbaijan and Georgia reached the open country north of the Caucasus. A combination of peoples under Russian command attempted to oppose them but the effort failed and the Khan's tribesmen won a great victory. This disaster, however, was not the beginning of the Mongol invasion of Europe; it was merely the curtain-raiser to the play which was to follow. Genghiz Khan recalled his army to Asia for his great attack on China, and thirteen years were to elapse before the real advance on Europe began. In the meantime, the factions in south-east Europe and Russia instead of healing their differences, closing their ranks and preparing to meet a new threat

[1] Born 1819. Called to the Irish Bar 1840. L.L.D. of Trinity College, Dublin 1850. Barrister, Gray's Inn, 1847. Q.C. 1868. Leading counsel for the claimant in the Tichborne case, 1873. Disbarred in 1874 for his violent conduct of the case. M.P. for Stoke-on-Trent 1875–80. Author. Died 1880.

should it materialise, continued to indulge in their quarrels and dynastic feuds. The interval of opportunity granted by God's grace became the years that the locusts had eaten. The blow fell in A.D. 1237, ten years after the death of the old warrior. The west was attacked under Batu Khan, one of his grandsons. The irruption this time occurred near the upper Volga launched due west from Siberia. South Russia felt most of the blow. In 1240 Kiev fell and destruction and massacre spewed over the Russian provinces.

An army with contingents from Prussia and other countries met the Mongols at Leignitz on 5th April 1241. The result was calamitous for the forces of Christendom. The Tartar masses spread like an avalanche over many parts of Europe burning and murdering as they went. It is not proposed to chronicle in detail the subsequent conquests which the Mongols made in Europe but when in due time they reached the Oder and the Drave they suddenly withdrew to their Russian territory and in A.D. 1260 at the death of Mangu Khan, 4th Mongol emperor, the princes of the league of the golden horde were sufficiently powerful to claim and attain their independence. Thereupon, they left the rest of Europe undisturbed and riveted their yoke on Russia till the 15th century.

The wanton destruction caused by the Vandals, Goths and Huns was a child's exercise compared to the havoc and ruin brought about by the Mongols whose lust for extermination passed the bounds of imagination. A further Mongol invasion of Europe occurred under Tamburlane in the early 15th century but as the firearm had been invented by then we are concerned neither with its course nor its consequences.

Tartar armies under Genghiz Khan were, like the Roman legion, planned on the decimal system. Over each ten horsemen was a *decanus*, over ten decani was a centurion, over ten centurions was a *millenarius* and over ten millenarii a commander called a *tomanbeg*. An army which might consist of several groups of 10,000 was led by two or three generals of which one was in overall command. Discipline was harsh in the extreme, the death penalty being meted out to anyone who showed the slightest trace of cowardice, regardless of his rank.

Each horseman carried two or three bows, three quivers, an axe and a stout rope for hauling vehicles. In addition, some had scimitars while others were armed with a kind of glaive for wrenching their opponents from their saddles. Their arrows were about $2\frac{1}{2}$ feet long with very sharp steel points which they kept in condition by constant filing. Shields were of wicker but few carried them as they were considered an encumbrance for horse-archers. The greater proportion of the troops wore helms, the upper part of which was of iron and the lower part of leather for covering the neck and throat; cuirasses of leather stiffened with bitumen; body armour consisting of overlapping leathern strips fastened by iron buckles; and cuissarts for guarding the legs and thighs. Their horses had leather bardings protecting them down to the knees and iron frontlets on their foreheads. Some of the more prominent leaders affected scale armour. It will be seen, therefore, that the golden horde was amply protected on the battle-field against injury or death.

When a Tartar force was about to attack it despatched a cover-ing screen of mounted scouts well to the front to act as an advanced guard for intelligence duties. Any information gleaned was sent back to headquarters. These scouts neither burned nor pillaged though for safety's sake they killed all they met. Behind this advanced body rode the main force which grabbed what it could, burned what it could not and slaughtered all and sundry. When crossing a river became necessary, each man placed his gear in a sack which he tied tightly to his horse's tail. When such packing was completed, the leading horse was urged into the river with a man to guide it. The first animal having taken the plunge the remainder followed with their owners often sitting astride their bundles. In this way the army could get to the opposite bank without the use of either pontoons or boats.

When the hostile force was discovered the Tartar hosts advanced to meet it and every man discharged three or four arrows. Should the enemy retreat at this first onset, the Tartars followed up in force to complete the kill. If, however, the enemy stood fast, the Tartars retreated and lured their foes on to ground already pre-pared with ambushes. If the enemy were foolish enough to fall into this trap, the Tartars retaliated and annihilated them. Should, however, the enemy prove too strong, the Tartars turned aside for several days' march and then burst forth into another part of the country to kill and pillage. Finally, if this plan failed, the Tartars would retire for ten or twelve days' march and lie up in some safe place till they thought the hostile forces had dispersed, when they would again sally forth to plunder.

When the Mongols resolved on a sustained action, the general with all the women and camp followers mounted on horses would take up a position well in rear of the fighting front. In addition, they placed dummy figures on horseback to create the impression that this body was a large reserve held in readiness in the background. The front line was formed of vassal troops strengthened by a few Tartar units. The main fighting strength was deployed far out on the flanks, if possible out of sight of the enemy. When the battle was joined the picked troopers on the wings closed in and attacked from all sides. This stratagem was to induce the enemy to believe that he was being attacked by an overwhelming number reinforced by a powerful reserve. Should the enemy put up a brave resistance, the Tartars opened their encircling ranks and let the enemy break through in order to make him think he was gaining the upper hand. Once the enemy had scattered the Tartars fell on them without mercy.

The Mongol method of conducting sieges was very thorough. On arriving at a hostile fortress they surrounded and even circumvallated it in order to prevent egress. They used engines of war and Saracen fire against their objective. Should these machines fail to secure their object, other methods including sapping and mining were adopted. If admittance were gained by such devices, one party set fire to the houses while the rest of the besiegers attacked the garrison from the rear. As a last resource for reducing the fortress, walls were erected completely enclosing it and the Tartars waited, maybe for months, for the place to be starved into submission. During the blockade, mild and tempting terms of surrender were offered. Should these unhappily be accepted, promises were broken and complete butchery followed.

The Tartars were without doubt unmoral, untrustworthy and treacherous but they were good soldiers blessed or cursed with a deep knowledge of strategy, tactics and duplicity. Apart from their savage customs, there were lessons in the art of war which European armies could well have learnt from their Mongol oppressors.

The heavily armed knights and the cross-bowmen of Europe were later to meet their match in the English longbowmen and for a time it looked as if England's troops would prove triumphant. The introduction of plate armour, however, tended to level out the position. This situation remained static till the Swiss re-introduced the phalanx in the middle of the 15th century. Deploying masses of men in close formation armed with 18 foot pikes, they again put the foot-soldier in the first position in action. These Swiss measures were successful for a time but they were in turn overthrown by the light Spanish infantry equipped with cuirasses, morions, small shields and swords and by the growing power of the gun, to which the phalanx presented so admirable a target. By this time, however, artillery was playing a more decisive role in war and the cannon and the firearm were becoming the dominant power on the battlefield.

CHAPTER XI

THE PANOPLY OF WAR

There has always been an association between colour and war up to the beginning of the present century, when warfare assumed a drab aspect owing to the neutral shade of uniform adopted by all countries. Up to a hundred years ago troops fought in full dress uniform and for an artist who could have concealed himself safely a battle would have provided a fitting subject. Three occasions in Britain used to demand full dress: church parades, field days and battles, and the first two undoubtedly provided enjoyment for the masses. In the British army, the Royal Horse Artillery, the Household Cavalry, the cavalry of the line, the Guards, the Highland regiments and the red-coated infantry added greatly to the panache of war and made hostilities resemble a review in Hyde Park. In the Middle Ages, the gaily caparisoned horses, the emblazoned shields and the crests of the knights supplied a touch of the circus to the art of fighting. War has always been a bloody business, but it became sombre only after the death of Queen Victoria when the sun had set on the rainbow of martial life. When chivalry with all its graces and dignity flew out of the window studied purpose entered by the door. Now the art of war has become a science and like all sciences it lacks the aesthetic charm of the arts.

The *standard*, which preceded the flag by many centuries, has undergone several changes of meaning during its long history. In England, the word at present means the flag emblazoned with the arms of Great Britain and Northern Ireland. This is known as the Royal Standard and being the ruler's personal banner is flown only when the sovereign is present. Originally, the standard was not a flag though it might have been mistaken for a flag-staff. It was a pole carrying a device rather after the style of a totem-pole. It typified the outward and visible sign of the inward and spiritual grace of the body or community it represented and might be compared to the ark of the covenant. In military affairs, it acted as a central command post, a rallying point for stragglers, a guarantee that the leader was still in being, a secure place of refuge for those momentarily worn out by fighting, a harbour for the wounded and a token that victory could still be achieved. It could almost be described as the *sanctum sanctorum* of an army in the field. It was therefore always heavily guarded by crack troops whose only mission was to prevent its capture at all costs. Owing to the mystical significance attached to the standard, its seizure by the enemy would confound and disperse an army because the soldiers would not know where to rally and would become dispirited fearing that their commander might have been taken prisoner or killed. Those in the rear being in ignorance of the facts would hesitate to advance against their foes. The disappearance of a standard therefore spelt disaster for the army to which it belonged.

The earliest evidence of a standard is derived from the primitive earthenware pots of pre-dynastic Egypt about 4000 B.C. These pots bore representations of a boat. This type of boat, apparently confined to the Nile, had two cabins amidships, and at the end of the after cabin a tall pole bearing an emblem is visible. The device on the emblem is thought to represent either their port of registry or the district in which the owner lived. All the different standards portrayed agree in having in their upper parts two hanging objects which appear to be long streamers attached to the pole. These standards were in due course developed into the nome standards of the Egyptian armies.[1]

The standards of the various ancient nations varied, particularly in regard to the devices they bore.

The standard of the Egyptians was an eagle stripped of its feathers.

The Greeks had no national banners but they had ensigns called *semeia*. The Athenian ensign was an owl on the top of a pole in honour of Athene, their protector; the Corinthian ensign was a pegasus or winged horse; the Messenian ensign was the letter M; the Lacedemonian ensign was an L; and the Theban ensign was a sphinx in commemoration of the monster overcome by Oedipus.

The standard of the Persians under Cyrus was a golden eagle with outstretched wings. The blacksmith's apron was used as a

[1] *British Flags.* W. G. Perrin. 1922. p. 6.

standard in 800 B.C. This is said to have been the apron of Kawah who headed a revolution against Biver.

There were four Jewish standards. A lion for Judah; a man for Reuben; a bull for Ephraim and the cherubim for Dan.

The military standard of the Romans, already outlined in Chapter IX, consisted of a silver-plated lance with a cross-piece on top which in some cases bore a small square flag (*vexillum*). From the ends of this cross-piece, whether it supported a square flag or not, hung ribbons with silver ivy leaves at the ends. Below these were a number of discs usually considered to be battle honours conferred on the legion to which the standard (*signum*) belonged. Below the discs was a crescent placed as a charm against ill-fortune. In the *signa* of the Praetorian guard crowns and medallion portraits of the Imperial House replaced the discs of the legions' standards. These *signa* were used as company ensigns to facilitate the tactical movements of the legion. The principal standard of the legion, corresponding to the regimental colour was the eagle (*aquila*). In the 2nd century B.C. there were five legionary emblems; the eagle, the wolf, the minotaur, the horse and the wild boar. Of these the eagle took pride of place. As that century neared its end, the custom arose of taking only the eagle standard into battle leaving the others behind in camp. Caius Marius, however, in his second consulship (103 B.C.) assigned the eagle exclusively to all Roman legions and abolished the remainder.[1]

The standard of Augustus was a globe, to indicate his mastery of the world.

The standard of Constantine the Great was called the *labarum* and its bearers were named *labariferi*. It was of purple material fringed with gold and was only unfurled when the emperor himself was in the field. This standard was decorated with the sacred monogram XP (*Christos*).

Vegetius records six types of Roman military insignia, i.e. *aquila*, *draco*, *vexillum*, *flammula*, *tufa* and *pinna*. The *draco* or dragon was adopted from the Parthians after the death of Trajan. It took the form of a dragon with gaping silver jaws fixed on to a lance. The body was made of coloured silk and when the wind blew down the open mouth the body of the beast became inflated.

[1] Pliny the Elder. *Natural History*. Book X 5(4).

The *flammula*, attached to a staff, was a long pennon split down the middle to form two streamers. The *tufa* seemed to have been a crest for a helmet and *pinna*, made apparently of feathers, was the name given to the side wings of the soldiers' helmets.

The standard of the Prophet was a green curtain. When Mahomet lay dying at Medina in A.D. 632 on the eve preceding the conquest of Syria, the chief officers entered the dying man's presence to receive his last orders. Ayesha, to save the Prophet from further exhaustion, tore down the green curtain which screened one end of the audience chamber, threw it to the officers and told them to preserve it as a rallying point for Islam. This standard floated over the walls of Vienna in A.D. 1683 but it was unfurled only in times of great emergency. In battle it was borne in front for all to see.

The Turks have two standards, one of green and the other of red silk. The former known as the Celestial Standard is the more important. It is a very large green silk flag said to have been given to the Prophet by the angel Gabriel. It is preserved in four coverings of green taffeta enclosed in a case of green cloth. The golden hand which surmounts the twelve foot high pole holds a copy of the Koran. This standard is housed and guarded with other so-called relics of the Prophet.

The standard of the Anglo-Saxons was an ensign carrying a white horse.

The standard of the ancient Danes was a fringed flag bearing a raven. It was often mounted on a wheeled stand.

The standard of the Franks was a tiger or a wolf on a pole. When they became Romanised they adopted the Roman eagle.

The standard of the Gauls was a lion, a bull or a bear on a pole.

In a battle with the Saracens near Acre at the end of August 1191, the banner of Richard I—a single lion—was borne aloft on a standard which consisted of a very long beam anchored to a solidly built platform bound with iron mounted on four wheels. It was made as far as possible proof against assault by sword, axe or fire. A picked band of soldiers guarded it against hostile attack or any other kind of injury. The object of the wheels was to facilitate movement so that the standard could be advanced or retired according to the state of the fighting and thus protect it from capture.

A somewhat similar machine was present with the English forces under Stephen during his fight against the Scots at Northallerton on 22nd August 1138 in which the English army prevailed. The machine bore a pyx containing a sacramental wafer and the three banners respectively of St. Cuthbert of Durham, St. John of Beverley and St. Wilfrid of Ripon. It was this erection which gave the name of *The Battle of the Standard* to this engagement.

Movable standards bearing emblems, ensigns or flags were thus not uncommon during the Middle Ages.

Armory and weapons sprang from a common source—the battlefield. Both may be said to have been born by necessity out of strife. The former comprises the rules and laws which govern the use, display, meaning and knowledge pertaining to the shield, the helmet and the banner. It is therefore a sub-division of heraldry which has additional implications including proclamations, ceremonies and matters of pedigree.

Armory can boast of an ancient lineage, its true origin being lost in the mists of time, for it evolved over the centuries from earlier systems of totems, signs, emblems and devices rather than emerged at any definite point in history. No particular individual can be credited with its introduction—like Topsy, 'it just growed'. It is generally conceded that the Crusaders were mainly instrumental in establishing a corpus of doctrine for armory. With earlier forms of armour, a certain amount of the knight's face could be seen, at least enough to ensure recognition; but when the pot-heaume became universal in the Crusade of 1190, hiding as it did the identity of the wearer, something had to be done. Not only was the man himself unrecognisable but even his nationality could not be determined. Therefore some distinguishing mark became imperative to identify not only individual knights but also their country of origin. Hence the introduction of crests on their helms and emblems on their shields which afterwards came to be recognised as the arms (coat or blazon) of the knights themselves. Since military leaders were all landowners under the feudal system, they tended to form the aristocracy of their respective countries. So the coats-of-arms they had assumed on the field of battle descended naturally with their estates to their heirs and became hereditary. Modern armory can thus be dated from the middle of the 12th century, when the custom of marking the banner or shield with some heraldic device appeared.

The seal of Philip of Flanders (A.D. 1161) shows the Flemish lion. The device of Philip Augustus of France was blue powdered with fleurs-de-lis. The Knights Templars adopted a banner, the upper part of which was black to spell damnation to their enemies and the lower part white to give comfort to their friends; while the Knights Hospitallers chose a red banner bearing a white cross. Even prior to this, individual kings had their distinctive banners, such as Harold who flew a red dragon and William the Conqueror who used a more intricate design.

THE TOURNAMENT

To complete this chapter, mention must be made of two military institutions which played a great part in England and the continent till the end of the 16th century. These were not battles in the strict sense of the word though they were sometimes lethal to the contestants. They were forms of games or contests which undoubtedly did much to stimulate and improve individual training.

The *tournament* was a spectacular display resembling in some ways a gymkhana or military tattoo. Its offspring today is the annual Royal Tournament at Earl's Court. The holding of military games in peacetime to accustom the soldier to the grim realities of war stretches back to the early ages of the classic period and spectacles of this type were not unknown in Rome. They eventually became general among most of the nations which emerged after the fall of the Roman empire in the west. France was a keen protagonist of such exercises among the main European countries. The tournament of the Middle Ages took the place of the popular sporting events of today, such as football, swimming, running and motor racing, for the contenders in the former had to undergo strict training and discipline in much the same measure as do the athletes competing in the modern Olympic games. It was also a popular event as it gratified the tastes of the military element and the upper classes as well as affording an insight into glittering pomp and magnificence to the otherwise dull lives of the less fortunate. In addition, it benefited financially the artisan who was frequently required to prepare the setting for this pageantry. Above all, it gave full reign to the mediaeval passion for cere-monial and display.

A tournament was an affair between contending teams, either from different parts of England or from countries abroad. The rules were strict and the programme was a set military exercise for which in some instances stage scenery was provided. The action which was fought with battle equipment was friendly though severe, as competition between the parties was keen. As a result, casualties often occurred, men taking part being killed or maimed. On this account tournaments were prohibited in England during the reigns of Henry II and Stephen, but later kings re-introduced them though the rules were tightened and more strictly enforced. It may seem extraordinary to modern minds that military perform-ances could be allowed in which knights and other nobles were sometimes killed, but they were no worse in this respect than motor racing at the present time in which crashes and death occur. One can be quite certain that more people suffer death and injury on our roads per month than were ever killed and maimed in tourna-ments per year.

THE JOUST

The *joust*, on the other hand, was single combat between two armoured knights armed with the lance. One contestant challenged the other to an affray for some form of prize. The rules were strict and etiquette was maintained. The gaining of prizes in jousting was settled as a rule by a system of points for and against, such as breaking a lance fairly on the body of one's adversary below the helmet, 1 point; above the breast, 2 points; and unhorsing, 3 points. Points would be lost by striking the saddle or the tilt. A lance should be splintered more than twelve inches above the head. In the tournament, too, particularly in the tourney or mêlée, fines were payable for certain offences such as maiming a horse. The modern equivalent of the joust is the professional boxing match, though it would be fair to add that the present purse for an international fight would far exceed any prize granted at a joust notwithstanding our depreciated currency.

Both these forms of military display were well patronised. The pageantry and colour were profuse and the occasion, especially the tournament, took on the bank holiday air of a modern Derby day.

CHAPTER XII

THE ART OF DECEPTION

Deception is as old as time itself and although Shakespeare tells us that 'Men were deceivers ever' they were by no means the first to practise it. The insect kingdom is a master in this particular art. Perhaps, the most perfect example of animal mimicry is that adopted by the stick insect to avoid its enemies. Ascending the ladder of life we have the moth, the external wings of which blend perfectly with the bark of the tree on which it alights, the sole, which identifies itself with the sandy ocean bed on which it lies; the chameleon, which changes colour to suit its background; and the tiger's stripes, which conceal it in its natural habitat to better its chances for stalking its prey. Other instances of camouflage in nature come to mind. The adoption of a white coat by the arctic fox and a similar transformation in the ptarmigan to conceal it in the winter snows, and the pantomime of a mother bird trailing an apparently broken wing to lead predators away from her nest.

In warfare, there are two main lines of deception practised: camouflage which, besides personal concealement, includes spurious battleships, guns, aircraft and equipment; and *ruses de guerre* i. e. operations of a tactical and politico-strategic nature calculated to mislead the enemy high command. Both these forms of trickery have been greatly developed in recent years and often require skill, much work and heavy expense to carry out. Before the introduction of gunpowder, however, there was little need of personal camouflage. When opposing armies paraded before one another within a few hundred yards, the object was not to hoodwink their foes but to prove their strength and numbers—a form of intimidation. Again, there were no dummy guns, ships or military machines. First, because the gun had not been invented and, secondly, because ships and military machines being comparatively easy to build, it was more profitable to construct the proper article than to make mock-ups which had no tactical or operational value. Doubtless occasions did arise during ancient sieges when dummy catapults were provided to dupe one side into believing that their opponents were more heavily armed than they were, but it is an open question whether such tricks played any useful purpose. Numbers in the old days being restricted, armies in the past could not afford to waste their limited manpower by manning useless facsimiles. Therefore only *ruses de guerre* need to be considered before cannon entered the world's stage.

When international law was unknown any trick was fair in war and ruses were generally made at the instigation of the local commander. Lacking telescopes, cameras and field glasses, clear vision in battle was limited to a few hundred yards and tactical movements on the actual field were easier to carry out. At 1,000 yards a woman on horseback could well be mistaken for a mounted warrior. The Tartar methods of hoaxing their foes when preparing for battle have been described in Chapter X and some of the frauds used in sieges have been outlined in Chapter III. To multiply such instances would be tedious as they followed no well-designed pattern and were the whims of engineers who thought them out on the spur of the moment. In any case, it is hard to distinguish between purely tactical moves and proper *ruses de guerre* in the field operations of long ago.

A special ruse may be illustrated at Dover castle. This majestic pile of fortified masonry on the south-east coast has many underground passages leading from one part of the *enceinte* to the other and from its central core to the outside world. In one of the latter types of passage the path led through a circular enclosure with a tipping floor. Below this floor is an oubliette the bottom of which was covered by a *chevaux de frise*, a wooden contraption armed with sharp iron spikes. During an assault, the besiegers, if they broke into this underground tunnel, would in traversing this hinged floor fall through and be impaled on the spikes below.

Another unpleasant form of deterrent was the caltrop, a piece of iron having four sharp points disposed in a triangular form like a tetrahedron, so that three of them always rested on the ground while the fourth assumed a vertical position. They were scattered over the ground in profusion where an enemy was expected to march, especially when mounted. This embarrassed their progress by maiming their horses.

The story of Macbeth as told by Shakespeare is well known, in which an apparition informs the former that he will not be vanquished till great Birnam wood shall come to Dunsinane. Macbeth scoffs at this and scouts the idea of a moving wood. Later in the play the messenger who comes to Macbeth and tells him that Birnam wood is on the move is called a liar for his pains. The real cause of this apparant movement was that Malcolm had ordered his followers to approach Dunsinane under cover of cut branches before closing in for the attack. When near their objective Malcolm tells his men to discard their greenery, Macbeth literally lost his head in the ensuing carnage.

History, however, gives another version. It states that Macbeth slew Duncan at Bothgowan near Elgin in 1039 and not, as Shakespeare avers, at his castle of Inverness. The attack was made because Duncan had usurped the throne to which Macbeth had a better title. Macbeth proved a just and equitable king but the partisans of Malcolm succeeded in deposing the former who was slain at Lumphanon in 1056. Shakespeare's tale, adopted from Boece, must therefore be taken with a grain of salt but it is an early example of tactical camouflage.

Frontinus[1] relates in his *Stratagematicon Libri IV* that Clisthenes, tyrant of Sicyon, blocked the aqueduct which supplied the town of Crisali. Shortly afterwards when the inhabitants were greatly affected by thirst he restored the supply of water but added hellebore which gave the Crisalians violent attacks of diarrhoea and this distressing complaint enabled him to capture their town.

The *ruse de guerre* which has passed into history as the master strategem of all time is the Trojan Horse. The story leading up to it is as follows.

Leda, the wife of Tyndareus, king of old Sparta on the river Eurotas, had an extremely beautiful daughter, Helen—'the face that launched a thousand ships'. Her true father is said to have been Zeus. When Helen arrived at marriageable age, her many

---

[1] Frontinus was a Roman of plebeian origin who became a praetor in A.D. 70. Five years later he obtained the command of Britain and was entrusted with the subjugation of the Silures. He was made consul in A.D. 74 and A.D. 97. In the latter year he was appointed general superintendent of the water supplies and aqueducts of Rome. Besides other works, he wrote a book on Roman aqueducts and the one on stratagems mentioned in the text. He died about A.D. 106.

suitors agreed that her choice of partner should be respected and that those rejected should band together to defend the rights of her husband whoever he should be. In due course, Helen married Menelaus, younger brother of Agamemnon, king of Mycenae. Meanwhile Paris, son of Priam king of Troy, had gained the favour of Aphrodite and gladly accepted her gift of the power of making himself irresistible to women. He visited Sparta and, during the absence of Menelaus, induced Helen to elope with him to Troy, leaving behind her only child, Hermione. True to their vow, the suitors gathered under the leadership of Agamemnon and sought justice for Menelaus. An embassy was sent to Priam demanding the return of Helen but it was refused. Peaceful persuasion having failed war was the only alternative.

After a lapse of ten years owing to several causes, the Greek expedition reached Troy and for another ten years laid siege to the city from the seaward side without much result as the land communications remained reasonably open. Despite the help of Ethiopians and other allies, Troy was at last reduced by a stratagem. Agamemnon pretended to withdraw his forces by sailing away, leaving behind him an enormous wooden horse constructed by Epeus in which were hidden some of his finest warriors. The Trojans, thinking that the Greeks had left for good, knocked a large hole in the walls of Troy and dragged the horse into the city thinking it to be an offering to Athena, their city goddess. Once the horse was safely within the defences, the picked men inside emerged during the night and helped by the pre-arranged return of their comrades quickly captured the city, during the taking of which many on both sides were killed including some of the leaders in this drama. Troy is said to have been destroyed on 12th June 1184 B.C.

Such is the Homeric legend. It is extremely unlikely that this episode ever took place though there is usually some basis for myth. Disentangling deities and humans, there may have been some wily move on the part of the ancient Greeks to eradicate a commercial rival. In any case, it is a story universally known and does illustrate the effect of a successful *ruse de guerre*.

CHAPTER XIII

WAR VESSELS AND THEIR ROLE IN ACTION

When some Paleolithic man first decided to journey down his local river he chose either a suitable tree and trimmed it to form a log on which to perch, or lashed together some stout branches to make a raft on which to squat. By this act, he made history. He became the original navigator and his unstable craft the prototype of the modern ship. For hundreds of millennia there was little or no improvement and the boat, if such a term may be applied, was used solely as a means of transport. The ship, i.e. a vessel capable of navigating oceans, came later and did not appear till the end of the Neolithic Age. Again, it was mainly employed for the carriage of goods and produce.

The fighting ship, a subsequent adaptation, was introduced for two purposes; to protect commerce on the high seas and to act as a troopship. Even when they became widespread, war vessels were not regarded as direct instruments of policy and the idea of a State having a nautical tradition did not exist. There could have been no conception in ancient Rome of an admiral as a bluff old seadog; the idea would have been quite foreign to the Roman mind. An 'admiral' commanding a battle fleet in one campaign could well have found himself the 'general' in charge of the cavalry in his next. At that point in history, the functions of a leader were the same whether he commanded on land or sea. There was, it is true, some slight sign of a naval outlook in maritime States such as Carthage or Byzantium but it amounted to little, and in the latter empire the navy was always considered the junior service. The notion, therefore, of an independent navy with its own corpus of discipline and loyalty was quite alien to contemporary thought. Man still regarded himself as a landsman and only took to the sea to arrive at a destination otherwise impossible to reach, and this view persisted till the 9th century A.D.

The oldest pictorial displays of boats, some of which are thought to be at least 6,000 years old, come from pre-dynastic Egypt. These vessels propelled by paddles were constructed from papyrus and had their masts well forward. They plied up and down the Nile carrying goods and food and were essentially river craft. Great care must have been exercised in handling them for they were extremely fragile. Their draught was shallow and their prows upturned to facilitate landing on shelving shores. After the accession of Menes, who is traditionally considered to have been the first dynastic pharaoh, boat-building became more formalised and wood as a material began to be preferred to papyrus. Egypt had little home-grown timber suitable for maritime purposes; only acacia and sycamore, neither of which was ideal for ships since the planks they yielded were both short and weak. Timber, therefore, was imported for the construction of larger vessels by 3000 B.C. as by this date the Egyptians had sailed out into the Mediterranean on voyages of discovery. River boats and smaller craft, however, were still built of indigenous wood. Sailing vessels by now had begun to show a marked improvement. The helmsman had a broader platform, the bipod mast had one forward and several after stays though no shrouds, the sail was braced by a man further aft and oars had begun to supersede paddles as an alternative source of motive power. The sail may have been sheeted but it is more likely to have been used like a modern spinnaker to enable the vessel to run before the wind. The ship was definitely beginning to compete with the boat in the maritime world.

Ramses III (1198–63 B.C.), the second king of the new dynasty, was the last great pharaoh of Egypt; a leader of capability and resource. During his reign he was threatened by a large force of Cretans, Philistines and other maritime Mediterranean peoples. The attack when it materialised came by both land and sea and was met with determined resistance. Ramses scored a notable success killing 12,500 of the enemy and taking 1,000 prisoners. Peace, however, was short-lived. In the 12th year of his reign another attack developed from the same quarter. This again resulted in victory by land and sea and the Egyptians were able to secure a more lasting peace.

Ramses III created the first naval force in history and his great battle—the first naval engagement—is commemorated on his tomb at Medinet Habu. His ships showed a great improvement over those of earlier generations for doubtless the Egyptians had learned much from their seafaring neighbours. All vessels at this date had a high washboard to protect the oarsmen. Whether Ramses's ships were ribbed is open to question but their general method of construction showed distinct advantages. The rigging was novel, tops were in evidence for the first time and sails could be furled without lowering the yards, a matter of considerable importance to fighting ships. After the death of Ramses III Egypt, the Ancient Light of the World, entered on a decline from which it never recovered. Occasional flashes of brightness lit the scene from time to time but the light was growing dimmer. The writing on the wall was plain to see and the final issue was never in doubt. The genius of the Nile valley passed into other hands and the country as a world power faded into obscurity.

The Dorians, a warlike people of ancient Greece, drove down from the north to the shores of the Aegean about 3000 B.C. They were a stern well-disciplined community whose conquests of, and subsequent dealings with, their foes resembled in many ways those of the Normans. Their war vessels, light craft of shallow draught, were in all probability large dug-outs not unlike the present-day war canoes of some South Sea islanders. Their build is largely a matter of conjecture but the strong sharp ram must have been integral with the robust easily-propelled hull. The vessels were fitted with outriggers to assist the work of the twenty-four oarsmen who supplied the motive power. Their dimensions were, probably, length 65 feet and beam 4 feet.

The Phoenicians were great seafarers devoted to commerce whose ships sailed the known seas in search of merchandise, penetrating even as far as Britain in their quest. Although primarily merchant adventurers, the Phoenicians had enough sense to realise that their trade had to be protected against the machinations of corsairs and pirates. They therefore built warships of the type known as the bireme for this purpose, i.e. a galley with fifty oarsmen seated in two banks. According to Assyrian bas-reliefs, the arms of the outer rowers were in a plane outside the upper deck supports and the hull itself was extended to bear the oars. The hull appears to have been hollowed out from a large tree trunk and thus belonged to the dug-out class. From this it may be surmised that the outriggers, i.e. the supports for the oars, were planked. The outer rowers thus sat on thwarts projecting from the hull into the outriggers. In this manner a narrow easily propelled hull could be retained, a straight fighting deck where soldiers could manoeuvre without upsetting the balance of the vessel could be installed, a higher speed and greater ram power could be maintained and, by planking the outrigging to achieve a reserve displacement, the possibility of capsizing would be reduced to a minimum.

By 850 B.C. galley crews became better organised and the galleys themselves radically altered so that they had a narrow fore-and-aft deck rather like the 'monkey-walk' in a modern tanker. This accommodated the fighting men, or marines as we should now call them, consisting of archers, slingers, javelin throwers, spear-men and swordsmen. These warriors were quite distinct from the oarsmen who with other 'naval personnel' formed the galley's crew. The galley still retained its ram of bronze or hardwood, the only form of naval armament then available. The oarsmen, unlike the criminals and slaves who rowed mediaeval and later galleys, were well treated and well fed for on the strength of their muscles depended the manoeuvrability of the war vessel in action. Whenever possible, sails were hoisted to conserve the rowers' strength.

An early naval engagement was fought off Corsica in 535 B.C. between the Carthaginians and the Phocaeans, a maritime people from Ionia in Asia Minor. The city of Phocaea was a great commercial centre and had during its long history become possessed of maritime ascendency in the western Mediterranean. The Phocaeans formed colonies, one of which was in Corsica called Alalia. After trouble with the Persians under Cyrus in their mother city, the Phocaeans as a body decided to emigrate, first to Chios and then to Alalia which they had founded fifty years earlier. They possessed long ships manned by fifty oarsmen which they had adopted from the Carthaginians and they seem to have been the first Greeks to have employed vessels of this nature. They remained five years in Corsica where they made themselves feared by their raids and acts of piracy on surrounding nations, so much so that they were at last challenged by the Tuscans and Carthaginians. The naval battle of 535 B.C. took place in the Sardinian sea and was a long and obstinate action. The Phocaeans succeeded in beating off their enemy, but they sustained such losses and their ships were so crippled that they abandoned Corsica and proceeded to Rhegium in Italy. In due course they were persuaded to settle at Velia in Lucania which in time became a flourishing city.

The Greek biremes of the 5th century before Christ were graceful vessels. They were of ribbed construction, a method of shipbuilding introduced by the Corinthians to supersede the earlier dug-out design. Their lightness and ease of manoeuvre was such that it is said that their crews could beach them, stern first, when occasion demanded. The keel was the backbone of the ship and it was further reinforced by a storming bridge which ran amidships fore and aft. From illustrations on contemporary vases it appears that the fore-post rose at the forward edge of the fighting bridge and that the ram may not have been an integral part of the construction but an addition which could be detached after a successful ramming without causing too much damage to the hull. The ends of the keel, wales, railing, outrigger lists and the rail on the helmsman's barrier were brought together and bunched at the stern. The vessel measured about eighty feet in length and had a beam of just over ten feet. The crew consisted of 25 rowers a side. These biremes were masted as the breadth of their beam allowed sailing with a minimum of danger. The sail was carried on a slender yard and could be reefed and furled with brails. The mast was probably lowered when the galley was rowed into the wind. This type of Greek warship improved substantially over the next hundred years. The seating arrangements, accommodating two rowers to each seat, were made more convenient. This added greatly to the ease of handling. The passage way between the fighting bridges was abolished and the vessel became completely decked. This 4th century bireme was about 65 feet long and 8 feet broad; it had a crew of fifty-two oarsmen.

The Greek *trireme* was a clumsier vessel, less answerable to the helmsman's wishes. Tiremes led to endless discussion among the maritime powers of the ancient world. Arguments for and against such unmanageable ships were long and heated. They appear to have been launched first in the 7th century before Christ. They had three banks of oarsmen. Two rowers sat side by side on the upper bank of thwarts and the third was placed in such a position that he could stretch his arms forward between the two oarsmen in front of him. The third rower's oar rested in a hole in the vessel's side while the upper bank of oars were seated on the outrigger which was planked above and below. The curved supports held up the fighting bridge probably leaving a sunken passage in the centre. When an attack was imminent the soldiers would be

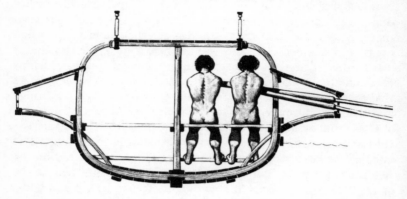

Fig. 52.—Seating arrangement for rowers in a bireme.

under cover in the passage and the rowers would be partially protected by the warriors' shields which were hung over the openings between the supports. The ram was integral with the hull, consisting in reality of the forward part of the keel reinforced by sturdy wales which ran together to a point. The three rows of oarsmen, known from the bottom upwards as the *thalamites*, the *zygites* and the *thranites*, had a hard task, but the hardest worked of the three were the thranites who had to pull on the heavy sweeps far up above the water. The trireme, though heavy and less manageable than the bireme, was a formidable craft moving at about seven or eight knots under the combined efforts of some 170 oarsmen. It carried five officers, thirty petty officers, a helmsman, lookouts and the *keleustes* who beat time on a gong or drum for the rowers. The vessel was fitted with a large lug-sail.

Even the trireme was not the largest vessel afloat in the ancient seas. *Quadriremes* and *quinqueremes* also had their being. The maritime Greeks at Syracuse constructed these mammoth ships. The

Fig. 53.—Seating arrangement for rowers in a trireme.

Carthaginians also had quinqueremes in their navy. As their names imply, these were four and five oar-banked galleys. The latter carried 420 men, 120 soldiers and 300 oarsmen and crew.

One might equate ancient and modern fleets as follows:

Quinquereme	Battleship
Quadrireme	Battle cruiser
Trireme	Cruiser
Bireme	Modern frigate
Single-banked galley	Destroyer

Roman warships followed the same pattern as the Greek, i.e. biremes, triremes, etc. There were also larger vessels in existence

Fig. 54.—Fragment of a relief in the Acropolis at Athens showing a section of a trireme. 5th century B.C.

such as *septiremes* and even greater. By the beginning of the empire, ships were completely decked with an open bow to secure internal ventilation. They had a tower which acted as a command post. The vessels had two sails, a main-sail and a small foresail, in addition to the rowers. The remains of two gigantic Roman ships, one a vessel of war, were found in Lake Nemi in Italy. Their dimensions were enormous; one was 235 feet long and 110 feet broad, the other 240 feet long and 47 feet broad. Why such colossi were built, who ordered them, who constructed them and why they were stationed on a lake must ever remain a mystery. Unfortunately, after excavation, their remains were housed in an Italian museum which was destroyed during World War II. One might consider them the *Great Easterns* of the Roman world.

Byzantium had a powerful fleet. The warship most favoured by the Byzantines was the *dromond*, a bireme with two or three masts carrying large lateen sails and holding between 100 and 300 men. In addition, they had a swifter bireme known as the *pamphylian* and a certain number of single-banked galleys. Byzantium had to maintain considerable naval forces to protect her commerce and empire, and tended as time went on to sacrifice displacement for speed as she realised that swiftness and agility were valuable assets in securing tactical success. Her great and much-feared weapon was Greek fire. This liquid, stored in cylinders, was pumped by bellows through a bronze flame-thrower situated in the bow of the dromond close to the ram. This mixture igniting on impact could be extinguished only by vinegar. As the ships were of wood, the results can easily be imagined. 'Ram and project' might well have been the motto of the Byzantine navy. There is no doubt that this devatating weapon was mainly instrumental in maintaining Byzantium's supremacy at sea for so long a period.

It is interesting to note that Byzantine naval strategy had quite a modern ring. Like the powers of today she abandoned the capital ship for those of a faster and lighter build in order to attain mobility and thereby secure the initiative.

The Scandinavians had been famous sailors and ship builders long before the Vikings became the terror of northern waters. Their vessels resembled those of ancient Egypt in that their bows and sterns were identical being ornamented with carved heads.

Fig. 55.—Byzantine warship of the 14th century. From a relief on a bronze door of St. Peter's in Rome.

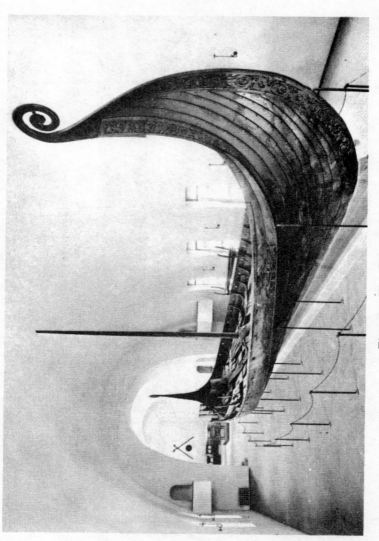

Fig. 56.—The Gokstad ship.

Fig. 57.—The Oseberg ship.

Fig. 58.—The Sutton Hoo ship.

In addition to their commercial craft, the Vikings had their warships called long ships; formidable vessels to encounter on the high seas. They were beautifully fashioned open boats with high prows and sterns usually adorned with gilded representations of dragons' and serpents' heads. They were built of oak after the fashion of a modern long boat but of much greater dimensions. They varied in size but some of the largest appear to have been almost 180 feet in length with stem and stern posts fifteen feet above water level. Exclusive of warriors, they carried some 68 oarsmen. Examples of Viking ships unearthed at Gokstad and Oseberg in Scandinavia and more recently at Sutton Hoo in England—where the vessel was found to be in an almost perfect state of preservation—showed no sign of rowers' seats so it may be inferred that removable benches were provided for the oarsmen's needs, and that their oars protruded through the sides of the ship. Great care was exercised in selecting the crew of a Viking warship, and as courage and determination were required to face the carnage of action, only those of noble birth and untarnished reputation were chosen. In addition to the oarsmen, these ships carried a sail amidships.

Illustrations in the Bayeux tapestry show that Norman ships were similar. Doubtless the Norsemen when settling in northern France took their ship-building technique with them. Alfred the Great built the first English naval force. His ships, based on Viking designs, were longer, higher, steadier and faster than those of his Danish foes. This was one of his great achievements by which he gained the rule of the kingdom.

Warships of the 12th century were developments of earlier types. The ram had been lifted clear of the water and the sails were more effective. Little further alteration had taken place by the 14th century. Byzantine ships still carried two banks of oarsmen, the upper bank resting on outriggers, the lower oars passing through the sides of the vessel. The anchor was a large grapnel of the type which persisted down to the 18th century. English ships of war of the 13th century had dispensed with oars and relied on sail except in calm water when heavy sweeps kept for such occasions were brought into use. They mounted two turreted castles, one forward and the other aft. A top castle on the mast was

Fig. 59.—Norman ships on the Bayeux Tapestry.

also beginning to emerge. It is evident that by this period warship design in northern latitudes was diverging from that in the Mediterranean.

What role in action did war vessels play over the long period under review? For much of the time naval warfare as such did not

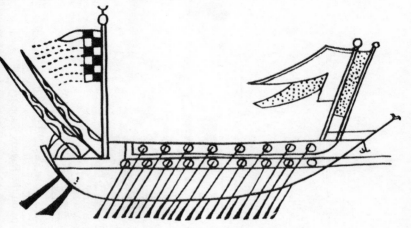

Fig. 60.—12th century warship.

exist, and the actions which took place were affairs between individual galleys. Any trading vessel was fair game. The technique was simple. Board it, exterminate the crew, seize the cargo and make a successful escape before reprisals could be taken. There were no navies in the strict sense of the term; galley fought galley indiscriminately. Both sides plundered merchantmen when conditions were favourable and raids on sea-port towns were carried out. The operative word was piracy.

Egypt was the first country to fight a naval battle and the engagement off Corsica between the Carthaginians and the Phocaeans may well have been the second, but struggles for supremacy at sea were rare. There was no overall strategic plan in these early sea-fights. Opposing galleys strove with one another and the nation which lost the greater number of ships was considered to have lost the battle. The absence of any signalling system would seem to have precluded any master plan. The first indication of concerted

From Valturius.—Edition 1472.

[Of this plate Valturius quaintly writes : ' When everything is cleared for navigation before the charge is made upon the enemy, it is well that those who are about to engage the foe should first practise in port, and grow accustomed to turn the tiller in calm water, to get ready the iron grapples and hooked poles, and sharpen the axes and scythes at their ends. The soldiers should learn to stand firm upon the decks and keep their footing, so that what they learn in sham fight they may not shrink from in real action.']

Fig. 61.—A ship of war; 15th century.

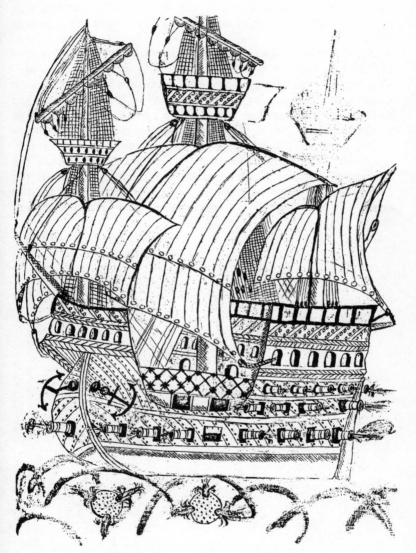

Fig. 62.—A warship; 16th century.

naval action appeared in Greek and Roman times and this was supplemented by the Byzantines who did have some vague notion of naval warfare.

The credit of conducting a real naval battle, as the word is now understood, must be given to Alfred the Great and the Vikings. The latter before engaging in battle, in which hundreds of long ships could be employed, lashed the bows of their ships together to form an unbroken line of vessels to oppose their foes. When battle was joined the ships hoisted their standards, blew their war-horns, unleashed a volley of javelins and arrows, and crashed into the hostile craft. Then under the terrific impact of grinding timbers the bloody business of hand-to-hand fighting began. This set the pattern for war at sea till the advancing power of artillery and the torpedo lent distance if not enchantment between the opposing fleets.

CHAPTER XIV

THE GREAT DIVIDE

There are times in the history of warfare when some new and unexpected agency manifests itself on the battlefield; not a mere change in conventional arms or organization but a novel conception which will revolutionise the art of war and alter completely the accepted mode of combat. The initial effect of its influence may be feeble, so much so that it will fail to affect the *status quo* for a long time; but the seed having been sown the harvest will be reaped. The more mediaeval an invention the longer it took to mature and in the Middle Ages none was slower than the cannon. Hatched as a puny weakling, it was rejected by the military minds of the period and scorned as an encumbrance, but it grew after years of adolescence into a weapon of vast potentialities. Its introduction led soldiers through a turnstile from which there was no return. Such a turnstile was the battle of Crécy in 1346.

For many years a controversy has raged as to whether or not King Edward III employed guns on that occasion. The arguments for and against this possibility have been admirably summed up by the late Lieut-Colonel A. H. Burne in his article *Cannons at Crécy*.[1] It was originally believed that cannon were employed by Edward in this battle, and that it was owing to the terror inspired by this new and frightening weapon as much as to the skill and prowess of the English archers that this country gained so signal a victory on that day. Subsequently, doubts set in and the idea that guns had been used in the field in such bygone days was discounted. It is of some significance to this survey that this vexed question should be settled, for if ordnance were indeed used at Crécy it would be tantamount to suggesting that field artillery had emerged at this early date. It would in fact, be the first authentic instance of such a role. Hitherto, the only reference to guns in action had been their employment at sieges and for the defence of towns and castles. The details of the battle are well known and it

[1] R.A. Journal Vol. LXXVII No. 4 p. 335.

is not proposed to dilate on them in this chapter, but before proceeding with a simple statement concerning the engagement it would be as well to glance at the armament supply side in England, as this throws some light on the question as to whether, in fact, guns were used by the English at Crécy.

We learn from Fleet's chamber account (25th January 1333–31st July 1334) that gunpowder and its ingredients were being used in England at this early date for military purposes. Robert Mildenhall's privy wardrobe account (17th October 1344–29th October 1351) also throws some light on the artillery position in this country. On 1st February 1345, Edward III ordered his privy wardrobe keeper to repair and ship all available guns and projectiles overseas for his projected expedition.[1] Little came of this but the preparations no doubt proved useful in view of the forthcoming Crécy campaign for on 1st October of that year Mildenhall was instructed to construct 100 ribalds for the king's passage to Normandy.[2] These machines were groups of small bombards in which the units could be either fired simultaneously or in rapid succession. The small barrels, assembled together and mounted in a single portable carriage fitted with two or four iron-hooped wheels somewhat after the style of a road sweeper's cart, discharged quarrels. Additional information concerning this order is furnished by the Issue Rolls of the Exchequer 1345–47 which show that between 10th October 1345 and 13th March 1346 Mildenhall was paid the sum of £124 18s. 4d. from Exchequer funds for the cost of these guns in eight differing amounts. On the assumption, therefore, that this account was not closed till the goods were delivered, it is reasonable to suppose that these ribalds were finished before the beginning of the Crécy campaign. Further evidence is adduced from these rolls that the work was carried out in the Tower of London by Crown artificers. The ironwork was fashioned by Walter, a king's smith, and Richard of St. Albans, the king's carpenter, prepared the woodwork.

On 4th March 1346, Edward III ordered the repair and shipment of certain guns kept at the Tower in the custody of Thomas Rolleston, a clerk. The latter, a subordinate of Mildenhall, clearly

[1] Pipe Roll 27 Edward III m 34.   [2] Pipe Roll 27 Edward III m 34.

had charge of the artillery for the 1346 expedition. The order reads:

'Guns with shot and powder for the same guns to be repaired and shipped. Ten guns with mountings, six pieces of lead, five barrels of powder, 100 large leaden shot for the same guns.'

In March 1346, 'powder for engines' was actually being produced in the Tower for the great wardrobe, in obedience to a writ of 10th May of that year, supplied Rolleston with 912 lb. of saltpetre and 886 lb. of quick sulphur for the 'work of the king for the use of his guns'. Further issues were ordered three days later. Obviously manufacture was proceeding apace since between 10th May 1346 and 15th September 1347 no less than 3,683 lb. of saltpetre and 1,662 lb. of quick sulphur were released from the great wardrobe to meet the needs of Rolleston and his band of powder-makers. These supplies were obtained through William of Staines, citizen and spicer of London[1] who was described in 1344–1345 as *apothecarius regis*.[2] About the same time money was being received by Rolleston from the chamber for warlike purposes. These and other entries indicate that the main purpose of these efforts was to supply a train of artillery for the siege of Calais, a siege which terminated in the fall of the town in August 1346. The part played by these bombards in the concluding phase is described by Froissart in his *Chronicles*.[3]

Further entries out of many obtainable from various wardrobe accounts between 1345 and 1347 give the following details:

1st February 1345	Guns with arrows and shot repaired and shipped for passage.
1st September 1346	All engines and guns in the Tower to be shipped; shot, barrels, saltpetre and powder and guns.
1st–2nd September 1346	Ten guns with mountings, two of which are large; five barrels with saltpetre and sulphur and other powder for the said guns. 73 large leaden shot; 31 small

[1] C.C.R. 1343–1346 p. 340.
[2] Enrolled Accounts (Wardrobe and Household) N. 3 m 42.
[3] Froissart's *Chronicles*. Johnes' Edition 1849 Vol. I cap CXLIV p. 185.

	shot; 6 pieces of lead for the same guns, were sent to Calais.
25th November 1346	750 lb. saltpetre and 310 lb. sulphur purchased.
15th September 1347	2,021 lb. saltpetre and 466 lb. sulphur purchased.

From this it can be gathered that the first three orders, namely those dated 1st February 1345, 4th March 1346 and 10th May 1346, were preliminary to the equipment for the expedition to France and prior to the sailing which took place in July. Therefore before Edward had left Freshwater he had shipped to Normandy ten guns with ten large leaden shot and half a barrel of powder for each gun; also six pieces of lead to make additional projectiles. Later on in May further quantities of the ingredients of gunpowder were bought. Some of these smaller pieces must have been present at Crécy. Edward took with him on this expedition a very small staff of technicians; namely six engineers, six artillers and six gunners, each of whom received a wage of 6d. per day,[1] now equivalent to 18s. This again presupposes cannon of a light portable type.

On 12th July 1346, Edward III landed at La Hogue in Normandy, devastated the countryside and returning northwards took up a strong position near Crécy. Both the English and French armies were divided into three divisions. There was a good deal of marching and counter-marching before the battle was joined. The two sides were well matched though the French infantry were rather a ragged lot being mostly untrained peasants. The strength of the French forces lay in their hired Genoese cross-bowmen, considered to be among the best archers in Europe. These, however, had had a long and exhausting march before reaching Crécy and declined to open fire as ordered. This angered the French commander who threatened them with death. A heavy thunderstorm broke out some hours before fighting began and the Genoese asserted that the rain had affected the cords of their cross-bows. After the storm had passed, the sun shone and dazzled the eyes of the Genoese who faced it; the English archers luckily had their backs to it.

[1] Harl. MS 782 fol. 63.

Hostilities eventually commenced on the late afternoon of 26th August 1346 and resulted in a great victory for England. Many Frenchmen of high rank including the King of Bohemia were killed. The number of casualties sustained by the French were heavy but the figure has been exaggerated by some historians. The crushing defeat suffered by France was in large measure due to the defection of their Genoese mercanaries.

Broadly speaking, those who deny the presence of cannon at Crécy base their evidence on the absence of any reference to artillery in this action in Froissart's *Chronicles* or in any of the writings of contemporary English historians. They argue that if guns had been present Froissart, the careful chronicler, would not have omitted to record such an important fact. To their minds this clinches the matter. Incidentally, in a later edition of his work called the *Amiens Edition* which came to light in 1839, he says:

'And the English kept quite still and discharged some canons which they had with them in order to disturb the Genoese.'

Finally, later in life, Froissart compiled a shortened version of his *Chronicles*, known as his *Chroniques Abrégées*, in which he wrote

'The English had with them two of the bombards and they made two or three discharges on the Genoese who fell into a state of disorder when they heard them roar.'

There are several possible explanations why this reference was omitted by Froissart in the first or *Valenciennes* edition of his *Chronicles* but they are not relevant to the point at issue.

However, Froissart was not the only continental writer interested in Crécy. The celebrated Florentine historian Giovanni Villani, who was noted for his integrity and meticulous regard to detail, asserts that Edward III during the battle of Crécy 'did mix with his archers "bombs", which by means of fire, darted small iron balls for the purpose of affrighting and destroying the horses; and that this kind of missile caused so much noise and tremour that it seemed like thunder from heaven, whilst it produced great slaughter amongst the soldiery and the overthrow of their horses'.

He also says:

'The English guns cast iron balls by means of fire. . . . They made a noise like thunder and caused much loss in men and horses. . . . The Genoese were continually hit by the archers and the gunners. At the end of the battle the whole plain was covered by men struck down by arrows and cannon balls.'

Villani died of plague at Florence in 1348 and therefore must have written a contemporary account of the battle of Crécy before the lapse of years had had time to dim his memory.

A history or chronicle was published by Muratori under the title of *Historie Pistolesi Dall'anno MCCC al MCCCXLVIII*. In the preface Muratori states:

'The author of this writing is unknown to us. He relates what occurred, especially in Tuscany, from 1300 to 1348. There is no room for doubt that he lived at this time, and probably the same pestilence which carried off Villani in 1348 and to which 80,000 people fell victims, destroyed the author of this chronicle. His history is even more minute than that of Villani.'

There is no doubt that Muratori had a high regard for the accuracy of the *Historie Pistolesi*.[1] In it occurs the sentence:

'The English knights, taking with them the Prince of Wales and many bombards, advanced to attack the French.'

Rapin says that the English first used guns at Crécy[2] and quotes Mézeray as his authority. Francois de Mézeray records:

'It is also necessary to point out that on this memorable day the English had four or five pieces of ordnance. It is thus proved without doubt that this was the first occasion on which these frightful weapons had been seen on our battlefields.'[3]

A passage in *Les Grandes Chroniques de Saint Denis* reads:[4]

[1] Muratori: *Rerum Italicarum Scriptores* Tom II Col. 516.
[2] Rapin's *History of England*. Written in French and translated into English by E. Tindel. London 1732. 2nd Edition Vol. I Book X p. 425.
[3] *Abrégé Chronologieuse de l'histoire de France*. Francois de Mézeray. 7 Volumes. Vol III pp. 26, 27.
[4] Cotton MS Nero E II Part 2 fol. 397.

'Thus the king with all his people assembled, went to meet the English, which English fired three canons by which it happened that the Genoese cross-bowmen who were in the front line turned their back and abandoned their fire.'

So much for the evidence of the written word.

At various times during the last hundred years small cannon balls of iron and stone, about $1\frac{1}{2}$ lb. in weight, have been unearthed on the site of the battle. These finds, though not in themselves conclusive proof, do in addition to the quotations given above, transform the probability into a certainty that artillery was used by Edward III and that, by the concentration of its fire on the unfortunate Genoese cross-bowmen, panic was caused among their ranks to the detriment of the French forces.

It is likely that less than half a dozen guns of small calibre were involved and that they were used at point-blank range in the capacity of mechanical projectors rather than as a separate arm. It is also reasonably clear that the effect of their fire was psychological rather than physical, for at the beginning of the 14th century fear of the unknown and unexpected was still a powerful factor in the morale of a battlefield.

Every age has had its Hiroshima.

CHAPTER XV

GUNPOWDER AND CANNON

The world has had many shocks and one of the greatest was in the 13th century when the introduction of gunpowder allowed the possibility of explosive force to be liberated from nature's powerhouse and caused a mild sensation in philosophic circles. It is true that the average man of that period had no conception of the vast changes such an invention would bring with it, and the experiments of those cloistered alchemists who pioneered this marvel left the Middle Ages unmoved. Yet its impact on society in general and on military art in particular was to be profound. It altered the balance of power, affected the fate of nations and changed the scope of warfare so that eventually war became a science. The only commensurable shock since that day 700 years ago was the release of atomic and thermonuclear energy at the end of the Second World War. The simple explosive of yesteryear has in our age unleashed a brood of Frankenstein monsters terrible to behold.

Explosives may be classified under three headings:

> Initiating agents
> Propellants
> High explosives

of which the second is that used for making up gun and rifle charges.

An explosive may be defined as a substance which, on being suitably initiated, is able to exert a sudden and intensive pressure on its surroundings. The term *explosion* is somewhat loosely employed in modern phraseology. An explosive body either truly explodes or detonates. Should it be susceptible only of the former, it belongs to the propellant or low explosive class; if it detonates, it is a member of the high explosive family and is used in mining or for filling shell. An explosion proper is combustion, i.e. a rapid oxidisation, the oxygen being drawn from the surrounding atmosphere. In other words, there is no distinction between the explosion of a mass of gunpowder and the rusting of an iron nail except in regard to the speed of oxidisation. A detonation, on the other hand, is a wave motion of the order of 4,000–5,000 metres per second throughout the mass, analogous to a sound wave in air or the transmission of a blow along a metal bar. A high explosive, therefore, must contain unstable chemical groups with an internal store of oxygen capable of being liberated by shock. A propellant is a more stable compound which if kept away from fire or sparks is relatively harmless.

The essential properties of a propellant are:

(1) A readily controllable rate of burning.
(2) An absence of smoke and residue after combustion.
(3) Freedom from flash.
(4) An easy liability to ignite.
(5) A non-erosive effect in the bore of the weapon.
(6) Stability in storage.
(7) Insusceptibility to moisture and temperature.
(8) Small bulk.

These characteristics are fundamental and it was, primarily, the failure to appreciate them and, secondly, the inability to procure them which gave rise to most of the troubles experienced with early artillery.

An explosion occurs with the liberation of energy when chemical action takes place between certain specific substances, and this untapped source of power must have been ever present in the minds of alchemists while reciting their magical formulae and bending over their alembics. Until, however, some mediaeval philosopher in his restless search after the unknown stumbled upon some propitious mixture this dream remained unrealised. Gunpowder was the first explosive discovered. There can be no doubt about this; all accounts attest the fact. Arguments and counter-arguments only arise over the question of its originator. Instrumental also as a high explosive, it was the only propellant in use for guns and firearms for the first five centuries of artillery and it held this pride of place until the introduction of smokeless powders in the middle of the 19th century brought its reign to a close.

Though a simple mixture, probably no substance has ever given rise to so extensive a literature or to so much death and destruction. Its origin is obscure and its invention has been ascribed in turn to the Chinese, the Arabs and others of the Muslim faith in the East as well as to other nations in Europe. Out of this welter of views, however, the name of Roger Bacon stands pre-eminent among those to whom the invention of gunpowder has been ascribed. He is a hot favourite for the 'Gunpowder Stakes' and may justly be termed the father of English gunpowder. The Chinese, Byzantines, Greeks, Arabs and Hindus were all familiar with compositions consumable on ignition which they used with varying degrees of success during the wars of the Dark and Middle Ages. The Chinese were certainly acquainted with saltpetre, the essential ingredient of gunpowder. They called it *Chinese snow* and used it early in the Christian era in the manufacture of fireworks and rockets. Nevertheless, a familiarity with this almost universal natural deposit does not necessarily imply a knowledge of explosives notwithstanding the fact that each one of the races mentioned has at one time or another been credited with the role of inventor. Modern scholarship, however, tends to show that all such combustible mixtures were incendiary rather than explosive in character and that gunpowder itself was not prepared before the 13th century, the most likely date of its introduction being between 1240 and 1249.

Roger Bacon was an outstanding personality far in advance of his time. Like Leonardo da Vinci, he was an intellectual giant reared in an age of superstition. He was born of well-to-do parents at Ilchester, Somerset, in 1214. He studied at Oxford under Grosseteste, graduated M.A., became ordained in 1233 and joined the University of Paris a year or two later. Paris at that time was the centre of scientific learning and Bacon's prowess in physics, mathematics and alchemy gained him the name of Doctor Mirabilis among his contemporaries. He returned to England and entered the Franciscan Order at Oxford in 1250, but his lectures aroused such a storm of indignation among his jealous and ignorant brethren that in 1257 Bonaventura, the General of the Order, placed him under strict monastic discipline in Paris for ten years. Pope Clement IV, who admired the erudition of the learned friar,

Fig. 63.—Roger Bacon.

instructed him to prepare a monograph on the prevailing state of science. This he did, and as a result of papal intervention Bacon regained his liberty and went back to Oxford in 1268. Ten years later, however, he was again imprisoned for his unorthodox views, his subsequent release being deferred till 1292. He died at Oxford about 1294.

Roger Bacon's work of most value in connection with gunpowder is his *Epistolae de Secretis Operibus Artis et Naturae et Nullitate Magiae* dedicated to William of Auvergne, Bishop of Paris, who died in 1249. If the dedication be authentic, the author must have been familiar with gunpowder before that date. The original text has in all likelihood been lost though two partial MS copies exist, one at the Bodleian and the other in the British Museum. The main theme of the discourse is an attack on magic, and in the earlier chapters arguments are adduced to show that science can accomplish greater marvels than the Black Art. It is a scientific thesis of a high order considering the time in which it was written. In the later stages Bacon describes what he evidently conceives to be the most wonderful truth of all, but, whether from considerations of personal safety or with a view to withholding dangerous knowledge from the ignorant, he writes under the form of a cypher or anagram. After Bacon's cypher had puzzled the world for centuries, the labours of Lieut-Colonel H. W. L. Hime (1840–1929) at last supplied the key and proved this farrago of apparent nonsense to be none other than a cloak for Bacon's recipe for the preparation of gunpowder and for his knowledge of its destructive force.

Gunpowder consists of an intimate mixture of saltpetre, charcoal and sulphur, the proportions of which have varied from time to time. In the dawn of artillery development the three ingredients were mixed as fancy dictated, the amount of each constituent being left to the whim of the powder-maker concerned. This laxity in an age when ballistic science was still in the womb of time can be understood. The main criterion for powder in the days of its infancy was its readiness to explode on ignition. So long as that could be guaranteed manufacturers and gunners were satisfied regardless of results. Roger Bacon's recipe was saltpetre 41·2 per cent, charcoal 29·4 per cent and sulphur 29·4 per cent. English gunpowder at present consists of: saltpetre 75, charcoal 15 and sulphur 10. These proportions were laid down in 1781 by Richard Watson, D.D., F.R.S., Lord Bishop of Llandaff, and have been adhered to ever since.

The earliest form of gunpowder, known as serpentine, consisted of particles in a very fine state of division. It suffered from serious drawbacks, the chief of which was its great liability to absorb moisture owing to the hygroscopic nature of the saltpetre. Other faults were a tendency to separate out into its component parts during transit, its large residue after firing, its need for very careful ramming, its characteristic of burning slowly when over-rammed instead of exploding and its property of giving rise to large quantities of explosive dust.

Several expedients for overcoming these disadvantages were practised. William Bourne in his *Arte of Shooting in Great Ordnaunce*, 1587, says:

'The powder rammed too hard and the wad also, it will be long before the piece goes off. . . . The powder too loose . . . will make the shotte to come off the mark. . . . Put up the powder rammer head somewhat close, but beat it not too hard.'

Early powder-makers added camphor, sal-ammoniac and gum dissolved in spirit in an effort to forestall separative tendencies. Thus the *Codex Germanicus* of the 14th century states:

'If you want to make a good strong powder, take 4 lb. of saltpetre, 1 lb. of sulphur and 1 lb. of charcoal, 1 oz. of salpractica and 1 oz. of sal-ammoniac and one twelfth part of camphor. Pound it all well together and add spirit of wine and mix it in, and dry in the sun. Then you have a very strong powder of which 1 lb. will do more than 3 lb. otherwise. It also keeps well and becomes better with time. . . . Where there is no camphor it crumbles and easily spoils. But the camphor holds all powder together and is also strong and quick in all powder, if one puts it in.'

Salpractica, a mixture of saltpetre, camphor and sal-ammoniac dissolved in spirits of wine, was made by scraping off the deposit formed after evaporating the resultant liquid. It was considered to develop power by introducing more 'air'.

The greatest defect in early powder was its property of absorbing moisture. It was often found to be damp and useless when required. Such a contingency could not be lightly dismissed as it rendered land and sea armaments impotent. To overcome this evil, resort was occasionally had to drying. Another method was to store powder in waxed canvas bags, a policy which obtained in Scotland in 1459. To prevent stratification and minimise the risk of premature explosion due to dangerous dust, the ingredients were often carried separately and mixed locally as and when required. To prevent excessive fouling Peter Whitehorne mentions that charges for certain cannon were enclosed in 'bagges of linen or paper'—an early attempt at the cartridge. It will thus be seen that the teething troubles of the infant art of artillery were serious and that only haphazard means of eliminating the obvious were employed till the more scientific methods of the 18th century began to appear. All these remedies were regarded as palliatives to overcome temporarily the drawbacks of serpentine.

Powder-makers knew the solution—corned powder—but they could not adopt it for cannon charges till gunfounders could cast weapons of sufficient strength to withstand the increased pressures it induced. This powder, made in definite grains, had been known since the 15th century being first used at Nurnberg in 1450. It had been employed in small arms in England before 1560 but its power and excessive cost barred its association with early ordnance. As, however, it is mentioned in Richard Wrighte's MS of 1563 it must have been considered in relation to guns in this country by the middle of the 16th century.

The following advantages were claimed for corned powder:

(1) It was much less susceptible to damp, especially when glazed.
(2) It deposited less residue after firing.
(3) It did not stratify during transport.
(4) It required less careful ramming.
(5) Owing to the size of its grains and consequent greater surface and air spacing, it was consumed so rapidly that there was little or no escape of gas through the vent. As a result, it had, weight for weight, $33\frac{1}{3}$ per cent more power.
(6) It produced far less dust.

The comparative strengths of serpentine, corned powder and modern gunpowder may be tentatively accepted as 57:75:100.

Who invented the gun? That question must ever remain unanswered. Its first appearance is shrouded in the haze of obscurity which characterised early writers when they attempted to explain unknown natural phenomena which they did not understand. Their language was often so loose and their words so mystifying that it is almost impossible to arrive at the truth of what they were trying to express. The gun was an instrument of warfare beyond their ken and their imprecision must be excused since they were incapable of dissociating in their own minds the new weapon from the military machine and an explosive from a fire-raising mixture. In truth, the cannon was awaiting new words in all tongues to portray its characteristics and until these could be coined confusion would be bound to occur. The gun was probably never invented in the strict sense of the term; it just developed in Europe from early experiments carried out by mediaeval alchemists. An explosive, in contra-distinction to an incendiary mixture, having been evolved, it is quite reasonable to suppose that some adventurous spirit during his researches did succeed in blowing a bung out of some container. The inquisitive mind is perennial; it was just as active in the 14th as it is in the 20th century. It has an idea, conducts a series of trials and a novelty appears.

There is no evidence to suggest that the idea of the gun originated in the East.

Since the late 15th century the invention of the gun had, until comparatively recently, been attributed to Berthold Schwarz, a reputed Franciscan friar of Freiburg-im-Breisgau. Little is known of this shadowy personage and ambiguity exists about the dates between which he was supposed to have lived. According to old accounts it is clear that 'Schwarz' was neither his secular nor monastic name. In early writings he is as often styled 'Bertholdus Niger' or 'Niger Bertholdus' as he is 'Schwarz'. It was doubtless a cognomen given to him in reference to his researches as he was reputed to be a *Nygermanticus* or Master of the Black Art, in other words—an alchemist. His real name was said to have been Konstantin Anklitzen (Angelisen). He was supposed to have died in prison in Venice in 1384. An Elizabethan document ascribed

Barthold le Noir Schwartz
Inventeur de la poudre et de l'Artillerie Allemand
de Nation et de l'Ordre des Cordelier de S.t françois

Fig. 64.—Berthold Schwarz.

to him the discovery of a detonating substance and goes on to relate how an accidental explosion during the course of his experiments gave him the idea of harnessing this force by placing the mixture in a tube with a projectile on top. This claim of Berthold Schwarz to have discovered gunpowder is now dismissed. Evidently in their day both Lieut-Colonel Hime and Robert C. Clephan did originally believe in the authenticity of Berthold Schwarz, for the former in his *Origin of Artillery* inclines to the view that a German monk did construct the first cannon in 1313; while the latter in his *Early Ordnance in Europe* considered that the suggestion put forward by several writers that the work of this Franciscan friar did lead to the invention of a mortar was not improbable.

The evidence on which Black Berthold's claim to have invented the gun rested is said to be found in a municipal MS of Ghent—*De Memorial Boek Stat Gent*—a memorandum book or journal covering the years between 1300 and a date in the 15th century. After a list in this book of the municipal officers for 1313 occurs this item 'Item, in this year the use of *bussen* was first discovered by a monk in Germany'. This with another similar municipal MS of the same city was examined by a Belgian antiquary, Monsieur P. A. Lenz about 1840 who informs us that *bussen* were originally tubes filled with incendiary matter which were thrown among hostile troops. Since these were known to have been in existence long before the date in question it has been assumed that the term *bussen* in these documents was used in its alternative sense, i.e. cannon or the German word *Buchsen*. The memorial book itself is now, however, under grave suspicion. There are several copies extant, and the late Sir Charles Oman inspecting the archives of Ghent in 1923 ascertained that the pertinent entry occurred only in the later editions; in the earlier ones it had been inserted as a marginal note by an alien hand probably of the 16th century. He also discovered that in the earliest MS in which this passage is to be found it was interpolated; the entry took place under the year 1393 and not 1313. The inference, therefore, is that in those editions where it had found its way into the body of the text, the carelessness of some copyist had inadvertently written MCCCXIII for MCCCXCIII thus invalidating the claim, since guns were familiar historically many years before the later date. The word 'inadvertently' has been used, but the error may have been made deliberately by a German scribe in order to magnify the importance of his own country.

This exposure shattered the claim of Berthold and negatived the earlier views expressed by Clephan and Hime. In fact, the former completely changed his opinion in his *Ordnance of the 14th and 15th Centuries* in which he concludes that Schwarz was an imaginary individual foisted on posterity by German authors for the sole purpose of claiming cannon and gunpowder as discoveries of their countrymen.

Berthold Schwarz has in turn been dubbed a Greek, a Dane, a Jute, a Brunswicker, a Welshman and a citizen of Cologne. This flitting personality, if he ever walked this earth, might well have qualified as an earlier incarnation of the Comte de St. Germain.

Although a portrait of him entitled *Berthold le Noir Schwarz, Inventeur de la poudre et de l'artillerie Allemant de Nation et de l'Ordre des Cordeilers de St. Francois* occurs in Andre Thevet's *Portraits et Vies des hommes illustres* published in Paris in 1584 from which a splendid reproduction was executed by L. J. Gole,[1] and a statue is erected to his memory in Freiburg, there is considerable doubt as to whether this monk-cum-alchemist ever existed. Felix Hemmerlin of Zurich (1389–1464) and other chroniclers wrote about him and his exploits, but the evidence regarding his birth and life history becomes uncertain when subjected to critical analysis. Like Christian Rosencreutz, he appears to be an anthropomorphic mirage of history. Berthelot in the *Revue des deux Mondes* rejected him, so did Kohler, while R. J. Partington[2] boldly asserts that this mystic philosopher is nothing but *un homme imaginaire*. He says:

'Black Berthold is a purely legendary figure like Robin Hood (or perhaps Friar Tuck). He was invented solely for the purpose of providing a German origin for gunpowder and cannon, and the Freiburg monument with its date 1353 for his discovery rests on no historical foundation.'

Having laid the ghost of Brother Schwarz and proved beyond reasonable doubt that the entry '1313' in the Ghent municipal

[1] *Monumenta Pulveris Pyrii*. Oscar Guttman. 1906. Figure 6.
[2] *A History of Greek Fire and Gunpowder*. J. R. Partington. 1960. p. 96.

archives is a forgery, let us turn our attention to the attack on Metz in 1324 which was the other early occasion when guns were said to have been in action. In this siege it is stated that the defenders made culverins, cross-bows and other warlike contrivances while soon afterwards William de Verey arrived on the banks of the Moselle in a barge containing serpentines and guns. Since the names *serpentine* and *culverin* were not coined by that date, Dr. J. R. Partington rightly concludes that the document in question is another forgery. The chronicles of Peter of Duisberg, which give meticulous details about the wars against Prussia from 1231 to 1326 including the capture of many castles, omit all reference to cannon, and in the continuation of these accounts from 1326 to 1410 only one mention is made of the use of bombards and that was in the latter year.

Thus any reference to artillery prior to 1326 must be either a deliberate falsehood or an error introduced by a historian who failed to distinguish a gun from a military machine.

So the insoluble conundrum 'When did cannon first appear?' still faces us. All that is known for certain is that the earliest representation of a gun occurs in England and the first authentic mention of such a weapon is found in an Italian document. German literature, on the other hand, dealing with artillery matters is somewhat later notwithstanding the efforts made by many Teutonic writers to prove that their compatriots invented not only the gun and gunpowder but other equally unpleasant tools of war.

The first illustration of a gun in England is contained in the illuminated MS of Walter de Millemete, dated 1326, presented to Christchurch, Oxford, in 1707 by William Carpender of Stanton, Hertfordshire. This treatise entitled *De Notabilitatibus, Sapienta et Prudentia Regum* deals with the duties of kings. The author was Prebendary of the Collegiate Church of Glaseney in Cornwall and chaplain to Edward III. Unfortunately, the text makes no reference to the weapon it so ably depicts. Why this is so is not self-evident. The homily, no doubt, was prepared by the chaplain for his royal master, and as the latter was a fine soldier, a keen gunner and a great leader in the field, the inclusion of the painting may have been ordered out of deference to him.

Fig. 65.—MS. of Walter de Millemete; A.D. 1326.

The gun in the Millemete MS, shaped like an Indian club or a Chianti bottle, could have been made of leather, iron or bronze; all three materials were used in primitive gun construction. This proto-cannon was known as *gonne* by the English, *vaso* or *schioppo* by the Italians, *pot-de-fer* by the French and *sclopus* by Latin writers. It is mounted on a four-legged stand. The gunner, dressed in a basinet, a sleeve-surcoat reaching down to his knees over a hauberk of chain mail, and ailettes ensigned with the figure of a lion or a dragon, is holding a priming iron in his hand in the act of discharging the piece which is loaded with a dart, quarrel or bolt, i.e. an iron shaft with an arrow-pointed head feathered with brass. The colouring of the picture is very precise. The gun and the head and feathers of the missile are bright gilt, as is the helmet worn by the gunner. The top of the stand is white, while its four legs are green. The complexion of the gunner is dark and his facial details are clear. Presumably therefore he is intended to represent a non-European, possibly an Arab. The ailettes are red so is the touch-hole of the gun. The sleeve-surcoat is green. The priming iron or igniter is white. The background of the scene is blue with white spots. Whether there be any significance about the colours or whether the artist had only a limited selection to choose from and just followed his own fancy is impossible to say. The fact that the arrow-head, the brass feathers and the gun itself are gilt does suggest that all these objects were made of bronze rather than of leather or iron. The shaft of the bolt is undoubtedly iron. The projectile is shown just leaving the muzzle, the gunner having obviously ignited the charge. It appears to be moving across the door rather than through it. This of course may be due to a lack of perspective. Provided the drawing is generally to scale and the gunner assumed to be of normal height, the gun would be about 30 inches long and the missile the same length. In any case the head of the missile would be projecting beyond the muzzle when loaded.

The first definite mention of cannon is in an Italian document of 1326.[1] A decree passed by the Council of Florence on 11th February of that year appointed the priors, the gonfalconier and twelve good men to name two officials who were to make iron bullets and

[1] *A History of Greek Fire and Gunpowder.* J. R. Partington. 1960. p. 101.

metal cannon (*pilas seu palloctas ferreas et canones de metallo*) for the defence of castles and villages belonging to the republic. Other documents of the same year quoted by Davidsohn speak of payment to Rinaldo di Villamagna, a master of bombards (master gunner), for manufacturing iron shot, casting guns and procuring gunpowder.

On present evidence, therefore, the year 1326 heralded the birth of artillery in the shape of a grotesque vase-like body. This primitive prototype had a short life. It is doubtful whether any were produced later than about 1350. They were unsatisfactory, inaccurate, dangerous and useless weapons and were cold-shouldered by the fighting man who still preferred his more powerful engine of war. The vaso was to its successor as the 'cat's whisker' was to the thermionic valve in radio transmission.

The original wrought-iron guns which superseded the 'pot' or 'vase' type were known as bombards, a word derived from *bombos* meaning a loud humming noise (cf. the bumble bee). Primarily squat in shape like a mortar they soon developed a more tube-like appearance.

They were made as follows. Wrought iron rods were lashed round the circumference of a mandril over which was passed a series of wrought iron hoops at white heat. These on cooling shrank on to the rods compressing them firmly together. Usually eyes were forged on one or two of the hoops to take rings which were used in conjunction with hempen rope to bind the piece to its primitive bed or 'carriage'. The chamber portion in the form of a jug with a short slender neck was then forged from the solid, the tapered end being fashioned to fit the breech. This double operation was necessary as the craftsmen of the day found it impossible to produce a barrel without a mandril; consequently, it had to remain open at both ends. The chamber portion which contained the propellent charge was kept in place by a wedge in a special extension piece.

Contrary to popular opinion, therefore, these original wrought iron guns of the 14th century were breech-loaders. So it is true to say that breech-loading cannon were introduced about 1350. Five hundred years were to elapse before breech-loading ordnance, as the term is understood today, became a reality and an additional

Fig. 66.—The Bodiam mortar. Early 15th century. Found at Bodiam Castle, Sussex.

thirty were to pass before the modern breech-loading type of gun became universal. The advantage which breech-loading conferred must have been obvious to the early gunner who was also the artificer who manufactured his piece. Thus, almost from the beginning of his trade the gunfounder sought repeatedly to put this idea into practice. As so often happens, however, man's imagination and inventive faculty outran his ability to manufacture, and it was this circumstance which deferred the development of breech-loading weapons for so long. Like many other mediaeval projects conceived before their time they passed into eclipse for half a millennium.

It can be appreciated, however, that these efforts of early gun-makers entirely failed to secure obturation, i.e. the prevention of gas escape from the rear of the gun. Such an escape from a 'chamber pot' must have been not only excessive but variable from round to round. This early type of cannon was thus both danger-ous and inaccurate in the extreme. No wonder guns on their first appearance were shunned by the armed forces of Europe. Even the civilian *gonner* who made and manned these treacherous con-traptions must have breathed a silent prayer and commended his soul to God before he prepared his priming iron to initiate dis-charge. In later models of the larger wrought iron cannon, the rear or chamber end though forged separately was firmly attached, probably by welding, to the barrel portion. In this manner some semblance of obturation was obtained. Obturation was *terra incognita* in the 14th century and was not made effective till Victorian times.

Casting, which succeeded manufacture on a mandril, presented no new problem to the gunmaker; he merely had to adapt the principles of bell casting to his trade. In fact, it was often the bellfounder who developed into the gunfounder as both were smiths by profession engaged on a similar type of work. The process was simple. A mould of clay mixed with certain ingredi-ents was formed so that its internal dimensions corresponded to the external contour of the gun to be cast. A cylindrical core of the same material strengthened by an iron bar made to the correct size and shape to fit the interior dimensions of the piece was inserted into the mould. Molten metal was then poured into the mould and allowed to solidify. When all was sufficiently cool the mould and core were broken up and the 'dead-head' of the casting cut off. The rough casting was then bored as required and the exterior rendered smooth by tooling. This method made muzzle-loading a necessity.

There was no suggestion of standardisation in early cannon production, each piece being fashioned at the whim of its maker. There are, of course, certain mathematical considerations which govern the sizes and types of ordnance. For instance, whether the shot be of iron or stone there is a definite relationship between its weight and diameter and the calibre of the piece. Thus a saker, for example, must have a very similar bore and fire an almost identical round shot in whatever country it is cast. But within such defined limits every master founder made his guns according to the dictates of his own fancy and embellished them according to his own artistic tastes. Artillery has a universal application and all guns must conform to a type and resemble one another except when a freak cannon is produced to satisfy the caprice of some exotic ruler.

The earliest mention of guns in England occurs in the City of London archives.[1] The record states *inter alia* that 'In the Chamber of the Guildhall there are six instruments of *latone*;[2] usually called gonnes and five *roleres* for the same. Also, pellets of lead for the same instruments which weigh $4\frac{1}{2}$ cwt. Also 32 lb. of powder for the said instruments.' These weapons are undoubtedly the *gunnae* mentioned in the Chamberlain's accounts which were delivered in September 1339. From this extract we learn that these cannon were made of latten (a hard yellow metal resembling brass), fired leaden balls and were moved on rollers. The use in the original of the word *vocitata* which means 'usually called' shows that even by 1339 guns had become comparatively well known. These particular pieces together with certain springalds, quarrels, etc. were provided by the City against an expected invasion by the French.

From a study of the privy wardrobe accounts it is clear that

---

[1] *Memorials of London and London Life in the 13th, 14th and 15th Centuries.* H. J. Riley. 1868. p. 205. 13 Edward III. Letter Book F, fly-leaf.
[2] Latone or latten; a hard yellow metal closely resembling brass. *Notes and Queries.* 3rd Series, Vol. XII has an exhaustive article on this metal.

the original gun projectiles were feathered darts or quarrels, in other words the same type of missile as were projected from the *balista*. These were succeeded by stone balls for large cannon and bombards, and by leaden pellets for small guns. Iron shot during the 14th century had made only a fitful appearance. Round shot, however, did not make feathered darts obsolete as the latter were still articles of equipment up to the reign of Elizabeth I.

It is perhaps well to stress again that the gunner of the 14th century was not a soldier but a civilian craftsman, who himself made the gun and served it in action. The ordinary foot-soldier of the period was incapable of appreciating the simplest technicalities and the mysteries of the artilleryman's art were quite beyond his comprehension. Towards the end of that century the first halting steps in the direction of standardisation became visible, for though guns were still being produced in the haphazard fashion peculiar to gunfounders of the time, a certain pattern was emerging. The tendency was to make larger pieces, though smaller ones were cast when ordered. This trend was the direct result of current military thought which considered siegecraft the greatest gift vouchsafed to the talented commander and the sacking of cities more important than the defeat of armies in the field. The spirit of the military machine still overshadowed the concept of artillery, restricted its possibilities and delayed its normal development as a third arm in warfare. Because of this legacy from the past it was only natural that the main effort of early artillery should be directed into this channel. When a battle of movement did take place guns sometimes played a minor part but their use in the main was confined to delivering missiles indiscriminately at the enemy after the manner of the war engine; their employment in a tactical role never entered the heads of the leaders. In practice, the gun was always subordinated to the archer and his bow while the fighting which ensued was overwhelmingly an affair of horse and foot. Mobility as an adjunct to artillery performance was a notion of the future and guns which did figure in field operations were both cumbersome in movement and slow in action: a double disability which stultified their possibilities. The reason for this strangulation of effort was the poor means of gun transportation which lagged in development behind the weapon itself. Until the former could be improved, the latter was bound to fail in its proper task. It thus becomes evident why the ingenuity and skill displayed by the gun manufacturer was mainly exercised in evolving massive cannon for the besieged and besieger alike. As a good business man, he was adapting his talents to suit his market by attempting to satisfy the needs of his clients.

The appearance of artillery on the world's stage introduced a further factor into the art of war and made new modes of attack and defence available to commanders in the field; an event which ultimately caused the whole notion of battle to be modified. It was the major break-through of the 14th century comparable to that of the splitting of the atom in our own day. This arrival created little stir in the military scene except for its novelty, noise and smoke, as its gestatory period was long and its development slow. It may be truly said to have suffered from the 'inevitability of gradualness'. For this reason the gun during its first halting years by no means took pride of place among the armaments at the disposal of the fighting man. It was often regarded as more of a hindrance than a help in the pursuit of victory, and its main value as a weapon at first was its power to terrorise the superstitious mind, for it was far less efficacious than the earlier engine of war. Even two centuries later Montaigne could write in 1580:

'Except for the noise in our ears, to which we will henceforth be accustomed, I think that it is an arm of very little effect, and I hope that we shall one day give up its use.'

Artillery was usually looked upon as an encumbrance. It was unwieldy, heavy to drag and far better left behind when serious fighting was contemplated. In the minds of some, it must have borne the same sort of relationship to the military machine that mechanisation does to the horse. Something vile and hideous threatened the chivalry and pageantry of the battlefield and was therefore to be abhorred. This discouragement was to a large extent fostered by the gentlemen of Europe who lived in an age when strategy and tactics determined weapons, not the latter dictating the former as in our own day. Besides the primitive gun being feeble in its effects, it was dangerous to the gunners who manned it. As before stressed, the initial success derived from its

*From a MS. of " The Chronicles of England," Vol. III.
British Museum*, 14 E. IV.

Fig. 67.—Fifteenth century artillery.

employment was largely psychological for the damage that the ordnance of the first half of the 14th century was able to inflict was far less than that occasioned by the *balista* and the catapult. We must realise that the cannon of yesteryear was totally unlike its counterpart of today. It was a short pot-bellied vase-shaped instrument weak in its effects, uncertain in its performance and perilous in its use. It bore about as much resemblance to the modern weapon as a homunculus does to a powerful athlete. It was a parody of things to come; a caricature from the hinterland of science.

It is impossible to draw any hard and fast line between the small explosive personal weapon, later known as the handgun, and cannon in the 14th century as the same nomenclature was usually employed in contemporary records to express both classes of fire-arm; many guns were so small that they could be fired from the shoulder on a rest. The handgun of the 14th century was merely a cannon in miniature. The distinction between the small arm and the gun is therefore not readily discernible in early European literature. Both were derived from a common source—the primi-tive cannon—and almost two hundred years were to elapse before the handgun as a personal weapon finally emerged from the sha-dows. Up to the 16th century it was regarded as a species of light ordnance, a hand cannon, manned by one or two men as circum-stances demanded; and though referred to as a *hangonne* that term does not necessarily convey the meaning we should attribute to it today. Thus the sense implied in a text is often ambiguous, parti-cularly in England where the long bow remained paramount till the reign of Elizabeth I. For this reason, writers may perhaps be inclined to assign an earlier date for the introduction of the true handgun, i.e. as the forerunner of the soldier's musket, than the facts themselves warrant. For example, an indenture said to have been drawn up in 1338 between John Starying and Helmyng Leget,[1] since denounced as a forgery, contains the following sen-tence 'La hulke appelle *X'pofre de la Tour* dont John Kygeston est meistre iii canons de ferr ove v chambres un hangone'. Does this sentence refer to a proper handgun? A Latin word *sclopus*,

---

[1] Roll T. G. I 1097.

also written *scopetus* and *scopetum*, was current in Italy by 1331[1] to denote a small bombard manipulated by one man. Such weapons were used by the Bolognese in 1360 in the attack on Casalecchio. Once again the same question raises its head. Are we in the presence of light mobile artillery or was this the weapon of the foot-soldier? The archives of Perugia in 1364 state 'Il nostra comune de Perugia fece fare 500 bombards una spanne lunghe', etc. Quite a remarkable number considering the year in question: but again is a handgun intended? Words have a way of undergoing a change of meaning during the passage of time. An inquisition taken in 1375 at Huntercombe asserts that one Nicholas Huntercombe, with forty other persons armed with 'haubergeons, plates, baconettes cum aventayles, paletes, lanceis, scutis, arcubus, sagittis, balistis et gonnes venerunt ad manerium de Huntercombe', etc. made an assault upon the building.[2] Mr. John Hewitt[3] observes that a body of men making a sudden attack on an abbey manorhouse would be unlikely to have had in their possession any kind of *gonnes* except handguns. This is of course possible but nothing in the text justifies such an assumption and the attackers might quite easily have procured one or two mobile pieces for their enterprise.

The first mention of a handgun in England which would constitute evidence in a court of law, and according to the late Professor T. F. Tout[4] the earliest reference to such a weapon in Europe is found in a writ dated 7th November 1388 which reads as follows:

'Et prefato Iohanni[5] . . . per manos vicecomtes Northumberland, j canonem grossum vocatum gunnum cum duobus capitibus in vno trunco, iij canonis parvos vacatos handgunnes, j molde de cupro pro pellotes in fundendis.[6]

---

[1] *Muratori Rerum Italicum Scriptores.* T 18c 176 (Quoted in *R.A. Proceedings.* Vol. V, p. 26).
[2] *Coram Rege.* Hil. 50 Edward III.   [3] *Ancient Armour.* Vol. II, p. 298.
[4] *Firearms in England in the 14th Century. English Historical Review.* Vol. XXVI, No. 104, p. 684.
[5] John Derby, chamberlain of the town of Berwick-upon-Tweed. He had previously been 'Clerk to the king's guns' from 1st March 1370 to 30th March 1374 (*Archaeologia*, Vol. XXXII, pp. 386–387).
[6] 'And to the aforesaid John by the hand of the Sheriff of Northumberland, one large cannon called a gun with two heads in one trunk, three small cannons called handguns, one bronze mould for casting shot.'

This occurs in the privy wardrobe accounts of Ranulf de Hatton.[1]

Although the cannon succeeded the engine of war, the descent is collateral rather than direct. The principle of the gun differs fundamentally from that of any form of military machine. It depends for its propulsive power on the expansion of gas caused by the combustion of some explosive material and is independent of torsional or gravitational forces. It is, in fact, a form of a temporarily closed vessel, one wall of which is weaker than the others and so inclined to give way under pressure. Thus the gun and its charge form one unit. Neither can function in a propelling capacity without the presence of the other, and the idea of a cannon would have remained still-born had gunpowder not been discovered.

The object of artillery is to inflict the greatest possible amount of damage on the enemy in the shortest possible time and this is accomplished with any given equipment in direct proportion to the excellence of the gunnery and the efficacy of the battery position; or to put it more tersely, to bring the maximum fire-power to bear on its objective with the minimum of delay.

To the gunner of the Middle Ages this truism would have been meaningless. Even had such a concept entered the minds of one or two of the more enlightened followers of St. Barbara, it would have been impossible to have put into practice. Imagination and foresight are one thing, achievement is another. Noise, smoke and all the features of a grand parade were our ancestors' idea of fire-power and in their view the greater the display the more efficient the outcome. To act the superman was ever uppermost in the thoughts of the gunner of old, for was he not a man of importance in war, a being set apart and superior to his fellows on the battle-field? It must be remembered that even as late as the 16th century the gunner's craft was regarded as verging on the miraculous and this was held to account for the profanity of the artilleryman's language all over Europe. Those who dabbled in infernal substances were said to partake of the devil. The more likely explanation was that gunners considered themselves a *corps d'élite* and

---

[1] Keeper of the privy wardrobe from 9th May 1382 to 16th January 1396 (C.P.R. 1381–1385 p. 114 and C.P.R. 1391–1396 p. 668).

Fig. 68.—Early drawings of bases and a robinet.

were therefore less disciplined than the ordinary foot-soldier. In our own literature Edmund Spenser and William Shakespeare both testify to the awe and terror inspired by the discharge of the bombard and the roar of the cannon and speak in no uncertain terms of their frightful effects. Since range tables at this period were unknown, and in any case would have been impossible to construct, the mediaeval master gunner, even if he had been aware of the tactical employment of artillery, could not have applied his knowledge for the whole method of firing was governed by chance. Each gunner was the captain of his gun, which was his pride and joy, and he acted strictly as an individualist. There was no idea of corporate action, of using guns as a team or even of exploiting them in conjunction with infantry or cavalry. Mass employment of artillery under an independent commander simply did not exist.

Artillery tactics did not begin to emerge till the latter half of the 17th century. This was owing to two reasons; the theory of investment and the unsuitability of equipment. The former which had controlled military thought for almost two millennia could be described as a hang-over from the age of military machines. The art of siegecraft which re-flowered in Byzantium after the collapse of Rome spread to the civilised parts of Europe and the Near East. This explains why the engine of war and its specific role continued to flourish on the mainland of Europe and why early walled cities are found on the continent. This did not happen in England. After the departure of the Roman forces from these shores in A.D. 436 all traces of military machines disappeared. Since the Saxons and Danes were unacquainted with these formidable instruments of destruction their conquests in this island did not disturb the *status quo*. It remained for the Normans to re-introduce such weapons into England and with them their sequel—the fortified castle. Defence rested on the invincibility of strongholds rather than on measures of personal safety. In mediaeval sieges the defender, secure behind his ramparts, ran little risk of injury or death. He was indeed unlucky if wounded by an arrow, injured by a bolt or crushed by a stone. His adversaries were pestilence and starvation and if he survived these he considered himself fortunate. On the other hand, should his castle fall disaster

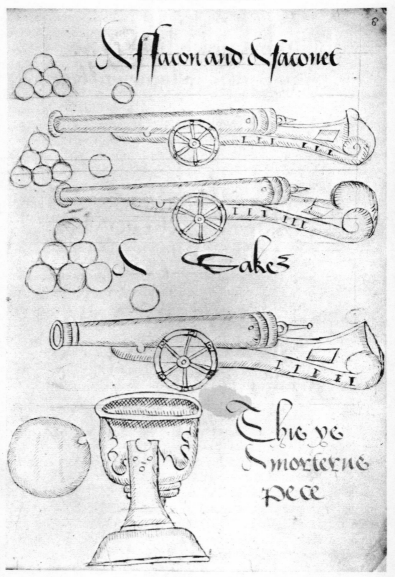

Fig. 69.—Early drawings of a falcon, falconet, saker and mortar.

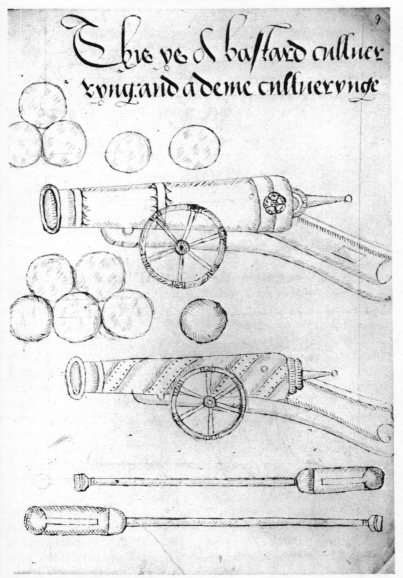

Fig. 70.—Early drawings of a bastard culverin and a demi-culverin.

overtook him. To gain his objective, therefore, the attacker resorted to more powerful machines. The reaction to this was the strengthening of existing works and the erection of more substantial castles and fortifications. Faced with the problem of reducing such centres of resistance the attacking commander somewhat naturally used his cannon as his predecessor had employed his military machine. The task was the same, merely the means of delivering the projectiles had altered. It can therefore be appreciated why the tactic of investment held the field for so long and stunted the independent development of the cannon for the first three centuries of its life.

The suitability of an equipment depends principally on the carriage of the gun. Till transportation improved and roads became lines of communication instead of lanes of mud—and it took the best part of 300 years to effect any progress in this respect—mobility, a necessary qualification for the successful employment of artillery in the field, awaited the 'kiss of life' by better methods of traction and metalled thoroughfares. The first man in Europe to appreciate the correct role of artillery in battle was Gustavus Adolphus of Sweden. Not only did he place the Swedish army on a more modern and enlightened footing, he also realised that mobility was a primary consideration where artillery was concerned. The ordnance of his day, divided roughly into siege and field, was cumbrous in the extreme. Even the 6 pounder field gun weighed half a ton and was mounted on the clumsiest and heaviest carriage imaginable. Once in action, it was almost impossible to extricate without an infinite amount of time, trouble and patience; commodities normally unavailable in the heat of battle. Gustavus, however, gifted with vision and a flair for equipment, went far beyond contemporary thought when he produced his light field piece, a 4 pounder weighing only 650 lb., and so lightly mounted that two men could handle it and one horse draw it. It was a momentous achievement. This weapon consisted of a metal tube frapped with coils of wire and covered with specially prepared leather, thus anticipating by 300 years a method of construction which did not come into general practice till the end of the 19th century. This new light equipment conferred a great advantage on the Swedes in the Polish War of 1626. The idea which germin-

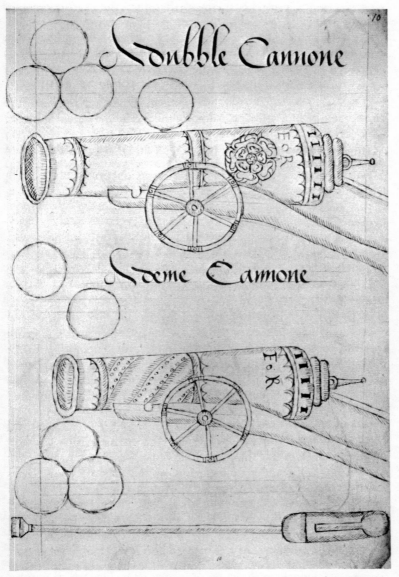

Fig. 71.—Early drawings of a double cannon and a demi-cannon.

ated in the mind of 'the Hurricane of the North' was applied with success by Marlborough later on in the same century.

Why the enlightened ideas and tactics of the Swedish king were not generally adopted by other nations at the time remains an enigma. True, most of their guns and carriages were cumbersome and their powder unreliable, but this clinging to shibboleths of a bygone age was a short-sighted policy. English writers of the period say little about the role of artillery in the pitched battle. They recommend that hostile guns should be captured by a rush as soon as possible and got out of the way so that fighting could develop in the orthodox fashion between horse and foot. They did agree, however, that cannon should be sited on high ground as a ball travelled with greater force downhill, though they were quick to point out that when pieces were depressed there was a tendency for the shot to tumble out of the muzzle.

In battle, the opposing forces were still being drawn up in line facing one another like toy soldiers. Such cannon as were present were dispersed between regiments of foot. Action was heralded in almost every case by an artillery duel, but one cannot help feeling that this was carried out more as a concession to time-honoured custom than as a means of influencing the outcome. In any case, such a duel was often curtailed by a cavalry charge with the result that the guns got caught up in the ensuing mêlée and were thus prevented from achieving their proper mission. When this happened the gunners were sabred and the guns captured as there was no means of rescuing them from the holocaust to take up a new and more advantageous position.

Gradually, ideas developed and in England both Cromwell and Marlborough introduced new measures to enable artillery to play a better and more suitable part. The Duke was first and foremost an artillery commander who personally took charge of the guns committed to his care. In this he showed a growing awareness of method till his employment of the great battery at Malplaquet proved his insight into tactics to be well in advance of his time. All his battles demonstrate that the Duke of Marlborough was a master in the art of artillery. Through him it is possible to observe how the use of artillery in war improved during the early part of the 18th century, and it was his genius which was responsible for

Fig. 72.—Early drawings of a basilisk and a bombard.

this progress in technique. Lord Wolseley considered that the Duke created the artillery as a separate arm and was the first commander to recognise this necessity. He could well be described as the father of the tactical employment of artillery.

Artillery thus took over 300 years to awake from its twilight sleep though at its awakening it still presented a pale image of its future to the world. It is true that between Queen Anne's time and the middle of the 19th century equipments gradually became better proportioned, less heavily constructed and more accurate, but there was little advance in basic design. Progress after the Crimean War, however, became rapid and continuous. Modern methods of breech-loading and recoil, rifling and manufacture, together with new types of sighting and independent rangefinders became established and set the pace for further improvements. These together with all the modern scientfic aids to gunnery and. precision have placed artillery in the predominant position it holds today.

EPILOGUE

Having completed this short survey what conclusions, if any, can be drawn bearing in mind that we approach the question from the standpoint of today. The conclusions would appear to be that:

(1) Man, though a reasoning being, is still influenced funda-mantally by an instinctive pattern of animal behaviour.

(2) Man can only gain moral stature under the spur of necessity. Remove that spur and he tends to become lazy and over-indulgent, and his resultant dissipation saps his vitality and turns his energy into inertia.

(3) Man learns nothing from the past.

(4) Satisfaction is the thief of opportunity.

(5) Nations follow man's path; birth, growth, fulfilment, surfeit, decline and death.

(6) Military organisations contain the seeds of their own decay.

(7) Attack is the best form of defence and the retention of the initiative is essential for victory.

(8) Strategy is cyclic.

(9) Peace depends on armed strength.

(10) Weapons are limited in character. Development can take place only within prescribed limits.

(11) Every weapon has its antidote.

(12) Conquest usually brings great scientific and architectural benefits in its train.

(13) The fellowship of man is still a distant goal.

Some of these conclusions may sound depressing but the study of human relationships, past and present, show them to be true. Has man ever appreciated the lessons of history? Can he follow a new path or must he for ever be conditioned by the past? Is he a free agent or is he caught up in some unknown tortuous web which compels him to conform to a cyclic movement? We see the events of the late Roman world mirrored in those of today. The arguments are the same, the actions are the same and the results will be the same. This seems inevitable because man apparently has no power of deviation. The wheel of fate spins in a spiral. Analogous conditions present themselves in a higher octave but reactions to them are similar and man behaves like a puppet on a string. The rivalry between weapons and their antidotes is ceaseless but as we move forward into an uncertain future the stakes, growing higher and more lethal, compel man to become more and more the plaything of circumstance. The latest folly of mankind is to install an anti-ballistic missile system, a defence arrangement which has been waiting in the wings to take its bow on the stage of actuality. The outcome of this is certain. It will be followed in due course by an anti-A.B.M. weapon. The process is endless until at last the world becomes a madman's paradise.

Aggression, a characteristic common to man and beast, is one of the basic evolutionary powers of nature. Without it neither development nor progress would have taken place. Tribal organisations, at whatever life level they stand, deteriorate and eventually disappear when their members cease to be aggressive. Fight and the world is with you, acquiesce and you die unknown. This is the great dilemma facing man today. If the human race is still motivated by the territorial imperative and continues to act aggressively, it may well perish in a thermonuclear holocaust; but should it abandon aggression it will sink into decrepitude and extinction. It is our Hobson's choice which can only be overcome by transmuting human aggression into divine discontent and concentrating on the future conquest of realms which transcend the mere struggles between nations. This natural law has overtaken the human race at last owing to its advanced scientific knowledge. The problem must be faced and the solution found without undue delay if man is not to perish from the earth.

Pope in a flash of genius exclaimed 'Man never is, but always to be, blest' and placed the emphasis on the future. The past should not be regarded as a series of events best forgotten but as a reservoir of human thoughts and endeavours which, if properly understood and digested, can point the way to that vision of the poet; a future not shackled to a treadmill but harnessed to the wings of inspiration, for profiting by the experience of others is the beginning of wisdom.

BIBLIOGRAPHY

The Antiquity of Man: Arthur Keith. Williams & Norgate, 1915.

Prehistoric Times: Lord Avebury. Williams & Norgate, 1913.

Downland Man: H. J. Massingham. Jonathan Cape, 1926.

Arms and Armour: Auguste Demmin. Bell, 1894.

Ancient Armour and Weapons in Europe (3 *vols*): John Hewitt. John Henry and James Parker, 1860.

A Critical Inquiry into Antient Armour (3 *vols*): Sir Samuel Rush Meyrick. Second edition. Henry G. Bohn, 1842.

Armour and Weapons in the Middle Ages: Charles H. Ashdown. George Harrap & Co. Ltd., 1925.

Arms and Armament: Charles ffoulkes. Harrap, 1945.

The Cross-bow: Sir Ralph Payne-Gallwey. Longmans, Green, 1903.

Projectile throwing Engines: Sir Ralph Payne-Gallwey. Longmans, Green & Co., 1907.

Vitruvius Book X: Loeb Classical Library. Vitruvius Vol. II.

A History of Greek Fire and Gunpowder: J. R. Partington. W. Heffer & Sons Ltd., 1960.

Military Architecture in England during the Middle Ages: A. Hamilton Thompson. Oxford University Press, 1912.

Mediaeval Military Architecture (2 *vols*): George T. Clarke. Wyman, 1884.

A History of the Art of War in the Middle Ages (2 *vols*): Charles Oman. Methuen, 1923.

The History of the Spur: Charles de Lacy Lacy. The Connoisseur.

The Flowering of the Middle Ages: Edited by Joan Evans. Thames & Hudson, 1966.

Military and Religious Life in the Middle Ages: Paul Lacroix. Dickers.

Encyclopaedia Heraldica: William Berry. Sherwood Gilbert and Piper, 18th century.

Byzantine Civilisation: Steven Runciman. Methuen, 1933.

British Flags: W. G. Perrin. Cambridge University Press, 1922.

The Tournament: its Periods and Phases: Robert Coltman Clephan. Methuen, 1919.

The Ship: Björn Landstrom. Allen & Unwin, 1961.

Sailors, Sailors: George Goldsmith-Carter. Paul Hamlyn, 1966.

Warriors' Weapons: Walter Buhr. Crowell, New York, 1963.

The Ordnance of the 14th and 15th centuries: Robert Coltman Clephan.

English Artillery 1326–1716: O. F. G. Hogg. R.A. Institution, 1963.

The Origin of Artillery: Lieut-Col. H. W. L. Hime. Longmans, Green, 1915.

Military Antiquities (2 *vols*): Francis Grose. London, 1786.

The Tower of London: William Benham. Seeley & Co. Ltd., 1906.

The Bayeux Tapestry: Collingwood Bruce. John Russell Smith, 1856.

Monumenta Pulveris Pyrii: Oscar Guttman. Artists Press, London, 1906.

INDEX